Acknowledgements

The research reported in this paper was carried out as part of a project entitled 'Cross-curricular Assessment Through Coursework for GCSE' and funded by the Schools Examinations and Assessment Council and the TVEI Unit of the Department of Employment.

The Project was directed by Paul Black and Robin Murray at the School of Education, King's College, London. My thanks go to them for their continuing help and support both in the carrying out of the research and in writing this book. Their comments on successive drafts were invaluable.

We were supported by a Steering Committee who gave helpful advice while the work was in progress, as well as commenting on draft chapters from this book. The members were: Graham Baker, Bob Bates, Chris Beesley, Andrew Cooper, Jennie Fordham, Dennis Griffiths, Rose Heatherington, Henry Mackintosh, Richard Mitchell, Jim O'Kane, Alan Quilley, Rachid Rkaina, Colin Robinson, Larry Sampson and Simon Sharp.

Support was given to me personally by a number of friends and colleagues. David Armstrong, Richard Bowe, Justin Dillon, Alister Jones and Shirley Simon all helped me in numerous ways. Pip Eastop was unfailingly patient and supportive during the writing up.

Finally, I would like to thank the teachers and students who gave up their time to talk to me about their work. I am particularly grateful to the four school co-ordinators who organised my school visits. Without them the work would have been far harder.

GW00600794

Contents

1 Introduction

This book is about what happens when teachers of different subjects come together to plan integrated coursework projects. It is about the ways in which the planning and assessment of such projects is affected by personal and group agendas, teachers' and students' perceptions of what they are doing, the management strategies used in the school and the influence of the assessment system. These issues are addressed mainly through the experiences of teachers in four schools, as described by them and observed by me, while they grappled with the complexities of combining work across the curriculum with the need to assess outcomes for separate subject examinations.

The multiple factors involved in carrying out interdisciplinary work for assessment purposes highlight a number of issues in what is often referred to as the micropolitics of curriculum innovation (Ball, 1987; Fullan, 1991). In particular, working across subjects brings out the intricacies and conflicts within and between subject-based teacher identities, which are not apparent when individuals work only in one curriculum area. The need to assess the work produced increases the importance of such identities because by forcing teachers to make explicit judgements about concrete instances, it drives them to be clear about what constitutes the essential elements of their subjects and exposes differences which are hidden by ambiguity in more general and abstract inter-subject discussions.

Why interdisciplinary work is important

A major advantage of an interdisciplinary approach to the curriculum is that it makes better use of students' time. By making it possible for one piece of work to be assessed for two or more subjects, it means that students are released from what can too often become a treadmill of coursework production, allowing them to spend more time thinking about what they are doing and produce higher quality work. Even with the 'slimming down' of the National Curriculum envisaged in the Dearing Report (Dearing, 1994), the curriculum, particularly at Key Stage 4, is likely to remain crowded; cross-subject work helps schools to take full advantage of whatever flexibility the limited time will allow.

Although a number of subjects will no longer be compulsory, and others need only be present in the form of short courses, it is probable that many schools will still want most of their students to study a broad curriculum, including some form of humanities, until the age of sixteen. As Dearing himself acknowledges, even if alternative accreditation can be implemented for the compulsory short courses in design and technology and modern foreign languages, 'many students will prefer to seek recognition of their achievements in short courses through a GCSE qualification.' (para 5.44). Although it is impossible to predict the exact outcome, this may leave schools with the alternatives either of insisting that students take full GCSE courses in these subjects, leaving the Key Stage 4 curriculum nearly as crowded as it was before, or of finding other ways by which these courses can be assessed. This can be done by two routes: students can continue to combine their short courses, or the work can be designed in such a way that it will contribute towards the assessment in a full GCSE subject or Units of GNVQ.

At the same time, students may well be taking vocational qualifications alongside their core studies at Key Stage 4. Although these will have their own means of certification, it is also important to consider ways in which work towards vocational qualifications can be incorporated into more academic curricula (Dearing, 1994 para 5.37). Dearing points out that students taking the core subjects plus a full GNVQ would have negligible time to study anything else; this means that if such students want retain breadth in their education at this stage, they will need to do so by completing work that can be certificated through more than one assessment route. Furthermore, in the GNVQ part of their studies they may take modules which are not based in traditional subjects. At the same time the coursework required for the non-GNVQ part of their education could be restricted to avoid overload. It would be much easier to approach such a combined curriculum through the use of cross-subject work.

Now that the National Curriculum requirements have been reduced at Key Stage 4, issues of relevance and transfer of learning across subjects will again come to prominence. In order to find dynamic and creative approaches to Key Stage 4, teachers will need to look closely at the curriculum and assessment requirements of their syllabuses, considering where there is overlap and how that can be used to make the GCSE experience more productive for students, in terms both of learning and of examination success. This book is based on extensive work in 29 schools and colleges in eleven English Local Education Authorities (LEAs), which then led to more detailed work in four selected schools, aimed at exploring, describing and clarifying the key issues in approaching cross-subject work. It focuses on the experiences of teachers when planning and carrying out interdisciplinary coursework, considering what was successful, what was less so, and why. It describes a wide range of approaches to cross-subject work, and shows how teachers can best reap the benefits of this style of curriculum management.

Background to the study

The work described in this book took place in the context of a National Curriculum development project, which involved 29 schools and colleges in eleven local authority areas[1]. The main aims of the Project were to work with teachers to develop interdisciplinary coursework projects for the GCSE examination, while at the same time liasing with the four English examining Groups to ensure that there would be no structural problems in multiple accreditation. At this level, many of the barriers to cross-subject assessment were removed, and the teachers involved were able develop a wide variety of approaches to the work (Murray, et al., 1994). However, the wide spread of schools meant that was difficult to see in detail what processes were involved in working with interdisciplinary coursework, so it was decided to focus on fewer schools in order to look at what was happening in much more depth. This detailed case study of four schools, conducted by myself, took place in the

---

[1] This was the Cross-Curricular Assessment Project (hereafter referred to as the Project) directed by Paul Black and Robin Murray and based at King's College, London, from 1988 to 1991. It was funded by the Schools Examination and Assessment Council and the TVEI Unit of the Department of Employment. I was the researcher on the project.

academic year 1990-91. It was mainly carried out through interviews with the teachers and students involved, observation of meetings, and some lesson observation, with the focus being on the way the teachers approached the work and how it developed from initial ideas, through carrying out the work with students, to assessment and moderation.

In all the Project schools there was an overall co-ordinator of the work; these were usually senior people, and several were already TVEI co-ordinators[2]. These school-based people were supported by a co-ordinator in their LEA, although, with the gradual running-down of the local advisory service during this period, not all schools were able to retain this support throughout the Project's work. In two of the LEAs involved in the detailed case study, there were support meetings between all the local Project schools, so I was able to observe these and check my findings against what was happening in other schools. This, combined with my continuing work in the other 25 Project schools, makes me confident in claiming that the processes that I observed are not peculiar to the four schools studied, but are generally to be found when this sort of innovation is undertaken.

A number of criteria were used to choose the four schools to be studied in depth. All of them had some continuing LEA support, and three of them participated in meetings with other Project schools, allowing me to have easy access to a wider sample. Although distant from each other, they were all sufficiently close to London to make it possible for me to spend whole days at a time in each school, making efficient data collection possible. They all had come quite a long way in developing cross-subject work, but by very different routes. This allowed me to meet the most important criterion, that between them they demonstrated a wide range of approaches, allowing different ways of working to be compared and contrasted as well as showing that very different teaching and management styles can be equally successful. Their reasons for undertaking interdisciplinary work were also very varied. Some teachers wanted to anticipate the National Curriculum by insisting that all students did at least some work in design and technology and modern foreign languages; they were interested in exploring ways of fitting in all of the National Curriculum subjects before it became compulsory to do so. Others were concerned that areas of the curriculum such as personal and social education (PSE), which had no examination outcome, had low status in the eyes of the students; they wanted to find ways in which the work done in these areas could be incorporated into assessed subjects. The issue of coursework overload was a widespread concern (Scott, 1990), and it was believed that one way to tackle this was to design pieces of work that could be accredited for more than one GCSE subject. Finally, it was thought that integrated coursework projects reflected more closely the world outside school, and that they might make it easier for students to transfer their learning across the artificial divisions between subject areas.

The work of the four schools has been analysed on a thematic rather than a school-by-school basis, allowing the various beliefs and practices to be compared and contrasted within a framework that focuses on processes rather than events. This reflects my belief that my findings not only have relevance in terms of the practices in the particular schools but are pertinent to the process of curriculum innovation in general. Thus not only do the themes on which I have chosen to focus arise from what I found in the schools, but these data are analysed and theoretically developed on the basis of the existing literature in this area.

Apart from this introduction and the conclusion, the chapters are presented in an order that approximately corresponds to the way that work develops in a school. I begin by considering what teachers

---

[2] Technical and Vocational Education Initiative. By the time the Project started work this was in its extension phase, which had interdisciplinary work as a specific focus.

and students think is involved in interdisciplinary work, and then look at the reasons why people take it on and the processes by which they decide to do so. Next, two chapters on the management of the innovation process look at the various ways that this was attempted and the advantages and pitfalls of each. With chapter seven, the focus moves to assessment, and the influence of assessment on teachers' subject subcultures; chapter eight develops this in looking at issues in assessed open work, the original focus of the Project. Finally, conclusions are drawn and suggestions made in the hope that teachers will be able to learn both from our successes and from our mistakes.

However, in order for the reader to orientate her or himself, it is first necessary to introduce the schools and the work they attempted. In outlining the projects set up by the four case study schools, I describe them here as they were originally planned. Of course, things did not always go as intended, but it is important to be clear what the schools set out to do, before discussing what actually happened. It is also intended to give an overview to which the reader can refer back during the more thematic discussion, so that it is not necessary to outline the projects in detail when discussing aspects of the work later on.

Lacemakers School[3]

Lacemakers School is a mixed, split-site 11-18 comprehensive in an east Midlands town. The school was one of the earliest to join the Project, and was supported in the LEA by Jennie Silcock, an adviser for the 14-19 age range, as well as by a support group of local Project schools. The school was in the process of making a number of curriculum and organisational changes. The staffing had been restructured, with the establishment of a team of directors of studies of equivalent status to the heads of English, mathematics and science, and who each had responsibility for reviewing the whole curriculum for one year group. At the same time, the timetable for Years 10 and 11 had been partly modularised, each module being approximately one term long, in order to give more flexibility for students to 'personalise' their routes through the curriculum.

The key to interdisciplinary work in the modular timetable was a programme of specially devised 'supplementary modules', taken in addition to students' normal GCSE courses. The school had moved from a 25 to a 30 period per week timetable. Each subject continued to have allocated to it the same number of periods as before, so there were now five lessons a week which could be used for other things. The senior management decided to take this opportunity to move closer towards the National Curriculum requirements by allowing (and in some cases requiring) students to take modules in subjects that were not part of their GCSE choices, the idea being that this would give them a more balanced curriculum.

Every student, therefore, had to take a module of personal and social education (PSE), combined with careers education, in each of years 10 and 11, as well as (over the two years) one of religious education (RE), one of music and one of modern languages. All students could be entered for GCSE integrated humanities by combining their humanities GCSE course (history or geography) with their PSE and RE modules and one module from the humanities subject not chosen as a main subject. Although these modules were free-standing and could be studied in any order, they were linked by a common theme. A further GCSE, in environment, could be taken by combining the full geog-

---

[3] The names of all the schools and teachers involved are pseudonyms

raphy course with modules from biology and either two or three supplementary modules (depending on the amount of biology being studied elsewhere) designed to pull the course together and fill knowledge gaps. Students could also use supplementary modules to follow up personal interests or to support work in areas in which they were weak.

All students (except those taking particular technology options, who had this incorporated into their course) also took a module of technology, taught by design and technology staff and supported for one lesson a week by a mathematics teacher. This provided the major piece of coursework for the mathematics GCSE. In addition, about forty students followed a combined arts course, which was staffed full time by one art and one drama teacher. This took up only the time of one GCSE subject plus one supplementary module, but led to examinations in both art (theatre design) and drama. The work for each subject was designed to lead out of the work for the other, and the final detailed investigation carried out for drama was in addition a major piece of art coursework.

Thus at Lacemakers there were three different strands of interdisciplinary work. The modular set-up allowed essentially separate subject work to be linked by a theme and combined to provide extra GCSE subjects, using coursework completed for the main subject courses to be credited towards integrated humanities or environment. In the technology/mathematics course one subject area provided a context for work towards another subject's examination, with the staff emphasising the links between the areas. Combined arts was conceived and taught as a fully interdisciplinary course, with each subject expert contributing as necessary.

At the same time, the school was moving towards an increase in interdisciplinary work in Years 7 to 9. It was decided that from 1991-92 the Year 7 students would have 20% of their timetable taught through integrated projects by members of the Year 7 tutor team. Although this was not the main focus of my study, as the negotiation for this was going on during the case study year, I did gather some data about the process as it went on.

The staff involved at Lacemakers were:

Bill Bailey	head of mathematics
Paul Barker	head of integrated humanities/history
Colin Fishbourne	mathematics teacher
Barry Johnson	acting head of CDT
Sheila Langden	head of drama
Martin Morton	assistant deputy curriculum and art teacher
Peter Panther	curriculum deputy head and school co-ordinator for the Project
Robert Partington	biology teacher
Roy Saunders	head of geography
Malcolm Standish	art teacher

Shipbuilders School

Shipbuilders School is a mixed 11-18 comprehensive in a medium-sized southern coastal town. Originally there was local support from two TVEE advisers, but both left during the case study year, leaving little subsequent LEA co-ordination. The school originally planned three strands to their interdisciplinary work. The first involved the designing and illustrating of books for young children, and was taught by the English and art departments. The project was started in English by asking the students to look at a variety of books for infant-aged children, considering the use of language, the sort of stories they contained, the type of illustrations and the relationship of words to text. Each student then chose a book to take into a local infant school and read to a group or groups of children. They also discussed with the children the sort of books they liked; the stories subsequently written were tailored either for a particular group in the primary school or for younger family members. At the same time, the art department would start work by looking at the nature of illustration of a variety of texts. Although all the English students wrote for young children, the art department allowed them to choose the age range for which they did their work; students therefore had the option of doing a joint piece of work or two separate pieces. When the stories were almost in final draft and some of the illustrations complete, they were taken back into the infant school and read to the children for whom they had been written, before being completed during the school (usually the summer) holidays. The books formed a major piece in students' English coursework folders, and were accompanied either by a 'learning log' (a step-by-step account of the processes gone through and the learning achieved) or an account of what had been done and why. Oral assessment was carried out by the English staff during the visits to the infant school. For art, the project constituted a full term's work and was thus a major component of the final assessment.

A second focus was on students attending the learning support department. In Years 10 and 11 a group of students took a 'support option' instead of one of their subject choices. In these lessons they were helped to carry out the coursework tasks that they needed to do for their GCSE subjects. The head of learning support, Hilary Blondel, used this opportunity to identify pieces of work that could additionally be used as English coursework pieces, either as they stood, or by adaptation.

The third project was aimed at the one-year sixth form. A link was planned between the information technology (IT) Royal Society of Arts examination and the GCSE in media studies, using the examination of newspapers, in particular the local press. Students were to survey the variety of newspapers available, and set up a database to store the resulting data. They would then study a local newspaper in more detail, again processing and presenting the data using IT. The impact on newspaper production of information technology was to be considered, as an illustration of the social and economic impact of information technology. Finally, students were to be asked to write and present a variety of articles for inclusion in the local newspaper. Unfortunately, this project never actually got off the ground, partly because of the logistics involved in the link with the local paper.

The staff involved at Shipbuilders were:

Rosemary Benbridge	head of information technology, science teacher and school co-ordinator for the Project
Hilary Blondel	head of learning support
Sally Brightday	head of art
Simon Hastings	head of media studies
Meagan Scanlan	deputy head of English
Donald Sidcup	head of English
Jenny Sims	English teacher

Stitchers School

Stitchers School is a mixed 11-16 comprehensive with a sixth form centre on the same site and sharing some staff. It is one of two secondary schools in a rural town in an eastern county, Camberside, in which Stonemasons is also located. During the Project it had support from a local science advisor, Tom Langden, and from a group of local teachers who met regularly to discuss cross-subject initiatives. The school had had a lot of experience of timetable-suspension, cross-curricular 'beyond school events' and co-operation between the home economics and CDT (craft, design and technology) departments.

The main focus of their work during the case study year was an integrated project involving geography, mathematics and science. This involved a group of about forty students who took part in a field course in Wales. Originally set up by geography as part of the GCSE requirement for that subject, it had been modified to incorporate work for both mathematics and science. There were two main foci: a river study (looking at various hypotheses concerning pebble size, velocity etc. at different points in the river), and a piece of work about the coast, which included an area of sand dunes. Science students were assessed on their practical skills as demonstrated in the field, and also carried out experiments using samples collected as part of the river study. They also did a number of species counts while doing their coastal work. The mathematics department used the statistical work involved to form part of students' coursework folders. An art teacher also went on the course to help the students with field sketching, although this work was not incorporated into assessed artwork.

The staff involved at Stitchers were:

Darren Cashman	art teacher
Kenton Clark	head of technology (former head of CDT)
Sarah Cordingley	head of mathematics and school co-ordinator for the Project from May 1990
Stephen Fieldwork	head of geography
Graham Peacock	TVEE co-ordinator, science teacher and originally school co-ordinator for the Project
Jeremy Paxton	geography teacher
Kevin Simons	head of integrated science

Stonemasons School

Stonemasons School is a mixed 11-16 comprehensive in a 'London overspill' town consisting mainly of a large council estate. Like Stitchers, it is in Camberside and was supported in the LEA by Tom Langden and the local teachers' group. The main concern at Stonemasons was the failure of many students to be entered for GCSE examinations because they had not completed their coursework. This was a problem right across the school, but was particularly marked in some areas, such as the CDT subjects. During 1989-90 a seconded teacher had considered this problem as the focus for his MA dissertation and had found that its roots lay in part in a poor student understanding of the nature of coursework and a general lack of ability to manage their time and resources effectively. It was decided to address these issues through the Flexible Learning Project[4]. The head of English had experience of this sort of work in her previous school, and she and a member of the geography department, John Blackwell, led the introduction of Flexible Learning methods into classrooms, with the support of the deputy head, Jim Branestawm and the TVEE co-ordinator, Gordon Swallow

---

[4] A TVEE initiative being carried out in several LEAs

(who also used Flexible Learning styles in their teaching), as well as an advisory teacher from Flexible Learning who spent several days a week in the school. The arrival of a new head in the summer term of 1990 gave the work further impetus; he was committed to the aim of raising achievement and saw the Flexible Learning Project, combined with a modularisation of course content (though not the timetable) as a key means to this end.

Interdisciplinary coursework was thus a second order goal at Stonemasons. It was believed that once students began to take control over their own learning they would see for themselves the overlaps between their subjects. Consequently there were no explicit cross-curricular projects in years 10 and 11 (some did take place lower down the school) although a number of individual pieces of work were carried out for two or more subjects, through teacher-student negotiation.

The staff involved at Stonemasons were:

John Blackwell	geography teacher
Jim Branestawm	deputy head
Pauline Hardy	head of English
Tony Higginbotham	headteacher
Gordon Swallow	TVEE co-ordinator and school co-ordinator for the Project

In both Stitchers and Stonemasons I also interviewed members of the newly formed design and technology departments as part of a related study. Although their comments are not quoted here, except where their remarks pertained to interdisciplinary work in general, they do form a background to my analysis.

A note on language

I started work on the Project when the National Curriculum was first being developed, and it was conceived well before then. At that time, the term 'cross-curricular' was not hung about with connotations deriving from the National Curriculum Council's 'cross-curricular themes', and, as it seemed to be the most widely used term, it was used in discussions with the schools and in interviews. Since then, however, I have found that when I talk about 'cross-curricular work', I am often understood to mean that done in the areas of citizenship, environmental or careers education, rather than cross-subject study as more widely understood. I think it is unfortunate that what was a good general term has taken on an unnecessary specificity; as a result, however, I have mostly used the alternative terms 'interdisciplinary' or 'cross-subject' instead of 'cross-curricular', although the latter term was generally used in interviews.

2 Interpretations of 'cross-curricular': who makes the link?

In approaching interdisciplinary work in the classroom, teachers bring to the task a wide variety of expectations as to what this will involve. Such expectations outline the ground on which they will work; they delineate the areas to which people direct their thoughts and affect what they consider to be good cross-disciplinary activity. The beliefs that teachers hold about what cross-curricular work is or should be lead to assumptions about what can be planned and with whom it might be organised. Such implicit definitions also affect the ways that they go about the process of inter-subject negotiation, and, given that (until they discover otherwise) people tend to assume their definitions are shared, this can lead to lengthy periods of misunderstanding before disparities in unstated meanings become apparent to all concerned. Furthermore, the assumptions held by the initial innovators in a school can set the tone for most, if not all, subsequent work, as they tend to be taken on board as part of a school-wide definition of cross-curricular activity. Students, in particular, may come to see as central, features that, for the staff, are peripheral to the activity; this can result in them failing to notice what the teachers intended as the point of the exercise, for example, that there are links and overlaps between subjects.

The term 'cross-curricular' is used in schools to designate a wide variety of different approaches and practices, amid a generality of unstated assumptions and failure to define terms. This was exacerbated during the period of the Project by the development of design and technology as a new subject from a group of previously separate areas (National Curriculum Council (NCC), 1990), the recommendation that information technology should be taught and assessed in context across the curriculum (National Curriculum Council, 1990) and the introduction by the NCC of five 'cross-curricular themes'. Thus, some teachers, who at the start of our work appeared at the very least to take on board our focus on common tasks devised to be taught and assessed by a number of subject areas, moved as time went on to a preoccupation with the provision of information technology across the school or to a major focus on areas of the National Curriculum not formally assessed, such as citizenship or health education. Furthermore, by the end of our time in schools, some of the cross-curricular themes, while starting out as areas around which departments might co-operate, were beginning in some cases to look as though they were seen by some people as subjects in their own right, taught by a discrete group of specialists.

Meanwhile, the requirements of assessment simultaneously pointed up and made more important the need for common understanding of what teachers and students were doing when they set out to design and complete cross-disciplinary coursework tasks. It became increasingly clear that some of the unstated assumptions held by the various people involved were not always compatible with the development of work that would be easy to carry out or to assess. Furthermore, what some teachers believed to be central to cross-subject collaboration was regarded as not being cross-curricular at all by others. All of this led to conflict and in some cases to project failure.

This chapter presents one particular way of analysing the data collected about teachers' and students' assumptions about cross-curricular work. In most cases the evidence is circumstantial or arises from open discussion of the work being carried out; I did not generally ask people explicitly for their definitions of 'cross-curricular' (although in some cases such definitions were volunteered). I have chosen to look at the data in terms of who or what, in each case, is perceived as working across the range of subjects involved. This is because it seems to me that beliefs about where the links are to be made are fundamental to the way that people choose to design cross-disciplinary projects; who or what does the linking determines to a large extent not only a further group of beliefs about the nature of the work, but also leads to specific assumptions and dilemmas about the ways in which it can be carried out.

Students

 Geography tend to see cross curricular as...[...]...being an idea which is reinforced in different areas...[...]...But the problem I think with that is it tends to be almost hidden curriculum and if it's too well hidden then the children won't appreciate it and at the end of the day they're the people who *have* to appreciate it, because it's just all hot air otherwise, something that teaching seems to suffer interminably from.

Darren Cashman, Stitchers School, 16/1/91

It is ironic that, while much of the current interest in cross-curricular work arises from a concern that students are unable to recognise concepts, skills or processes arising in several subjects, the resulting projects tend to leave such links to be made by the students themselves[5]. In many cases, the only people who actually worked across the curriculum were those who were believed to be least able to see possible connections, the teachers remaining in their discrete subject areas and contributing to the wider whole from this standpoint. Of course, this is also one way of describing what traditionally happens in secondary schools; in a subject-based curriculum, students move from one area to the other over the course of a day or a week and make links where they can (this may be why students find it so hard to tell that anything has changed when cross-subject work is carried out in this way). In projects where the students basically bore the responsibility for such linkages, this remained the case; the teachers saw their rôle primarily in terms of enabling such connections to be made more easily.

This was shown most clearly at Stonemasons, where the school placed great emphasis on increasing student independence in general. They were encouraged to use teachers as consultants, working out what they needed to know and whom to ask about it. There was also an stress on the cross-disciplinary nature of resources, which may have contributed to students' ability to see that they might obtain help from one subject to carry out coursework in another. For example, one student did

 a piece of work on pollution and I think a geographical survey as well as a science one, and a lot of the techniques that he needed to actually go out and test the nitrates in water and for testing for algae and all the rest of it we got from the science, because he went up

---

[5] I am indebted to David Armstrong for this observation.

there, they provided him with all the litmuses and all the different papers and chemicals. So we got a lot from there. In fact I was reading one last night, I was trying to mark, and they've actually said thank you to the science department for providing me with this and showing me how to do this, and they said thank you to the English department for helping me to put my work in this order and thank you to the geography department for whatever, it sort of came across, all the different sources that he'd actually used, so that wasn't too bad.

John Blackwell, geography teacher, Stonemasons School, 25/1/91

However, this was not the case in all schools. Darren Cashman, an art teacher at Stonemasons, expressed the commonly held view that students find it hard to make links between subject areas:

 I'm aware that the children had done tessellations, but when I taught them about repeating things it was like they had never heard of it. You know, similar problems between CDT and art in that I teach them to draw, but when they go down there it's like they've never picked up a pencil before.

Darren Cashman, Stitchers School, 16/1/91

The unstated assumption that it is the students that will form the cross-curricular links is associated with a thematic approach to the work. It is assumed that students will be enabled to make such hitherto elusive connections between subjects, if departments focus their work around an overarching theme. This may be devised to strengthen otherwise tenuous cross-subject links, as with the local community theme at Lacemakers, which formed the only connection between the various components of integrated humanities that did not arise simply as a result of their being geared towards the same examination. At this school the use of common themes to link very disparate subjects led to an almost jigsaw-like approach to the cross-subject work. In particular, Peter Panther, the deputy head, tended to use phrases like 'that all slots together' and talked about subject areas 'fitting in'. Thematic work may also arise from a desire to make more meaningful topics that are being covered in more than one area, with teachers contributing their particular expertise:

 For example the history department, they do first world war. It would be super if then, at that time we did first world war poetry...[...]... I could do the poetry with them, and it would really boost their subject tremendously and then they could give the nitty gritty instead of me having to teach them how the first world war began, and giving them some background, or the Russian revolution with Animal Farm, all these types of things you see.

Pauline Hardy, head of English, Stonemasons School, 22/11/90

However, the links between subjects were often still not made explicit to the students, with the result in some cases that they were unable to see any connections even after the work had been carried out. At Stitchers, where geography and science had basically worked on separate tasks alongside each other in the first year of the Project, the students' minds were instead focused on what for them was the most salient connecting feature of the work, that it was a field course. This seemed to limit their ability to think of cross-subject links in any other terms. While they perceived links, they could not operationalise this understanding outside the immediate context:

CP: But with the trip you'd said you'd got an extra piece of maths coursework, that sort of, you know automatically. Can you think of anything else that would do that, so that you wouldn't have to do extra work but you could count a piece for two things if you did a little bit of work on it? Is there anything else you've done that that would work for?

CDT...but there's nothing really you could do with CDT.

CP: Why's that?

It's not a sort of outdoor trip sort of area, is it, really, you've got be there in the workshop.

Year 11 student, Stonemasons School, 16/1/91

The teachers at Stitchers seem to have assumed that by carrying out related tasks in a common context, they would convey to their students the relationships between the subject areas in which the tasks were based. This does not seem to have happened in practice, maybe because the tasks themselves were always clearly 'for geography' or 'for science'. Similarly, the teachers at Shipbuilders involved in the children's books project assumed that students would understand the methods (for example in planning artwork) they were expected to use, as they moved from one subject to another, carrying with them an internalised idea of what was required for art, even when not in the art room. Again, this was not generally the case, students being influenced largely by the beliefs of whoever was teaching them at the time, though this was never a specialist in both subjects.

It is clearly insufficient, then, to expect only the students to work across the curriculum, unless they are given considerable support, as at Stonemasons, in developing generally applicable independent study skills. Students will not see links between subjects just because they are presented to them without comment; they are too used to viewing tasks as coming from discrete subject boxes. Although the use of themes may make the curriculum seem less bitty, and may give a more coherent 'feel' to the work from the point of view of those planning it, it does not seem to make an appreciable difference to those who have to carry it out, and may, indeed, distract them from making the more important linkages between the knowledge and skills practiced in different areas.

Teachers

In some cases, it was the teachers that formed the links between subjects by working across the curriculum themselves. The most radical proponent of this was Simon Hastings, the media studies teacher at Shipbuilders, who wanted to abandon class teaching altogether:

We've got to go down this road of cross curriculum and I asked [the head] if we could almost dismantle media studies as an examining subject and let me just become an umbrella, almost suspend completely then my timetable and then I would feed in all the lessons that I could think across, and I could go to CDT and give talks about products, cartons and how they're actually produced for certain audiences. We'd go back through all the stereotyping and all those other things, those other criteria which are important to me, and if a kid produces a new carton for a Weetabix packet or something, that could then be just as credited for CDT as it is for media studies. So I'd still be doing the examining bit, and the kids would be doing media studies as an examining subject, but within their subjects, rather than the media one.

Simon Hastings, Shipbuilders School, 10/1/91

In practice, however, no-one worked in this way. Teachers were timetabled either to team-teach or simply to work with whole classes in other subject areas. At Stitchers, Darren Cashman, an art teacher, taught CDT to one Year 7 group and supported another in textiles, as part of the art department's contribution to design and technology. At Lacemakers, the CDT-based technology/mathematics module was supported for one lesson a week by a mathematics teacher, while the combined arts course was entirely team-taught, staffed by both art and drama teachers. In this latter case, although all the activities were related to both subjects, they remained discrete until the final pieces of joint project work.

> There isn't really a mix in the lessons, I mean the lessons are either drama or theatre design. I don't think there are any lessons where they do both.

Malcolm Standish, art teacher, Lacemakers School, 4/6/91

Each subject specialist remained responsible for their own area, although the drama teacher felt that (after several years working like this) she had gained enough art expertise to teach the entire course if necessary.

The head of learning support at Shipbuilders worked across the curriculum in a different way. She saw her rôle as being to support individual students in making links between their GCSE subjects, by rewriting pieces of work completed in one subject area to be suitable for assessment in another. In general, she identified the links and helped the students alter their work accordingly, so any sense of the interdisciplinary nature of the work came through her.

> The music one, that's been fairly successful in that the composition, the actual wording was written exactly the same for music as it was for English, all that was needed for English was a sort of introductory paragraph about.... I mean this particular boy is an Elvis Presley fan, tries to dress like him and relate in any way possible, and he wrote actually a really good introductory piece about why he's an Elvis Presley fan, something about the history of him, and he mentioned that he enjoys some writing, he likes to write in memory of Elvis and all the rest of it, and then sort of his final line is 'and this is an example of some of my songs', and he included those.

Hilary Blondel, Shipbuilders School, 4/2/91

However, even when such work is done on a very small scale, there can be problems both with skills and with subcultural understandings on the part of teachers working outside their usual subject bases. Darren Cashman, the art teacher at Stitchers who worked in both CDT and textiles, was particularly aware of this and saw it as a difficulty for the development of design and technology.

> You see, the problem that we have, or the problem that we're finding with the so called cross-curricular work is that we're having people who are not necessarily skilled in one area, they can do some of it, but there comes a point where they find that their skills make it totally impossible for them to teach the kids something useful.

Darren Cashman, Stitchers School, 16/1/91

This concern was echoed by Peter Panther, the deputy head at Lacemakers, who felt that there was a danger that teachers would plan less rigorously when working outside their subject bases.

 what we don't want is just a catalogue of things which take place...a load of PSE based activities...I don't want that.

Peter Panther, Lacemakers School, 2/10/90

A further development at Lacemakers was departmental claims on the NCC cross-curricular themes. This was most apparent in the planning for the cross-curricular block in Year 7, where particular groups felt that they had the expertise to teach certain areas.

 Unfortunately the only people who are really making moves at the moment are science who are making massive claims and waving around the health education, you know.

CP: 'We teach the whole curriculum.'

Yeah, 'we teach the whole curriculum. This is it. This is going to be a topic', you know. And I said, really it's negotiable, you know, we're not giving it to you, it's not yours - we didn't intend that science should have sort of 30% of curriculum time - it's there for negotiation.

Peter Panther, Lacemakers School, 2/10/90

At the same school, the two teachers who had been responsible for the development of the GCSE Environment course similarly saw themselves as the local experts on the subject and were disappointed that they had not been invited to plan its inclusion into the Year 7 work.

There are benefits to be gained from teachers working across subjects themselves, the most important being a fuller realisation of which links can be made without undue strain. This understanding is crucial to the planning of work which will enable students to see such connections; if they are left to find them alone they will tend not to do so. However, if it is only the teacher who actually works in more than one subject at a time there is a danger that the students will continue to see subjects as discrete and the teacher as simply a specialist in several areas. For example, Darren Cashman found that although he taught the same students for both CDT and textiles, this did not enable them to see the connections between the two subjects that the move to design and technology should have made explicit. It thus appears that it is insufficient for either teachers or students alone to make the cross-disciplinary links; both need to do so, if there is any hope that the intersubject interconnections will be understood.

Same or Parallel Tasks?

The question of who makes the cross-subject link, the teachers or the students, is associated with a further debate about whether to do one piece of work that can be assessed for both subjects, or to carry out parallel tasks within the same theme or context. This debate was particularly intense at Stitchers in connection with the planning of the mathematics/science/geography field trip, especially as regards the link between science and geography. The first year they ran the joint course, there was an attempt to share most of the work done, students being assessed for practical science while making the measurements they needed to do for geography, although some additional science experiments were carried out in the evenings. However, unresolved differences in approach had, in practice, led to difficulties in doing this (see chapter 8), the resulting friction making subsequent negotiations rather tense. It was only at this stage that it became apparent that the teachers centrally involved saw cross-subject collaboration in fundamentally different ways. This was explained to me by Kevin Simons, the science teacher:

> You see what has happened now, as I mentioned before, what geography is trying to do is say well we will do our geography bit here and you can do your science bit there. And that's not the idea I don't think of cross-curricular work.

> *Kevin Simons, Stitchers School, 31/10/90*

While the head of geography, Stephen Fieldwork, saw cross-subject work as being parallel tasks carried out around a theme, both Kevin Simons and Sarah Cordingley, the head of mathematics, felt that it was important that the same tasks were carried out. Kevin, in particular, felt that unless this happened, they were not really doing cross-curricular work.

> I don't want to go there and do science and then do geography. I mean, it's a cross curricular project, surely the idea of it is that we do the geography and the science and the maths area of it all together

> *Kevin Simons, Stitchers School, 31/10/90*

Sarah was hopeful that this would indeed be the case the second time around.

> So the science is actually going on during the day, and so is the Geography. It's not so much that it's less Geography it's just it's going to be, they're going to do the same task, doing it the scientific way.

> Sarah Cordingley, Stitchers School, 17/5/91

Despite lengthy negotiations between the three departments, this was only partially borne out in practice (see chapter 8). Similarly, at Lacemakers, teachers contributing to the integrated humanities and to the environment GCSEs were gradually moving away from coursework tasks that could count for more than one subject and towards asking students to carry out separate pieces of work on the same topic.

> Some of the departments that work with an option to double assess actually choose not to do that. But rather add an extra piece of work which they assess just once. Now why they do that I'm not quite sure.

> *Peter Panther, deputy head, Lacemakers School, 2/10/90*

In both schools the use of parallel as opposed to joint tasks seems to have been connected with a reluctance to change one's current practice. At Lacemakers, it was largely teachers who were not fully committed to the course (mainly those in integrated humanities) or those (mainly in environment) who found the logistics of dual assessment difficult to cope with who did this. At Stitchers, the geography department, whose field course it had originally been, found their ownership of this very difficult to give up, for example, continuing to do all the administration themselves and being reluctant to give the other staff involved such things as lists of those going and a programme of activities. During this time, the department felt under threat from the National Curriculum proposals for humanities and were very concerned about what they considered to be the integrity of their subject and the importance of features seen as exclusive to it. For the science assessments to work, the geographers would have had to alter their normal practice quite considerably, as well as recognising the overlap between the two subjects; these they were not really prepared to do. Hence their proposal that there should be parallel activities.

The idea of doing the same work for both subjects is, on the other hand, associated with a holistic view either of students or of learning.

 It's just the problem I think of the twentieth century, we really...you know, and it sounds a bit grand, but this is the problem with the twentieth century. If we were talking in six-teenth century Italy this wouldn't be a problem because there was nothing strange about Piero della Francesca being interested in maths, but also being an artist.

CP: Yes, Peter being the Leonardo of Lacetown.

Right, and whereas we're trying to do these kind of things in an environment which for the last fifty years in state education has been geared primarily to a subject based curriculum, and we're just trying to cut across that stream.

Martin Morton, assistant deputy head, Lacemakers School, 30/1/91

 Teachers that work in narrow curriculum areas and just see their own subjects as the be all and end all of everything, I don't think are ultimately good teachers. They don't teach the whole kid.

Graham Peacock, TVEI co-ordinator, Stitchers School, 4/12/90

Actually achieving this holism in practice can be difficult unless both teachers and students work across the subjects involved. At Lacemakers, the combined arts course was treated in this way. Although the staff led teaching in their separate areas, they did all the planning together and there were always teachers from both subjects present in the lessons. For example, one student said, refer-ring to the two art teachers involved:

 They come into the drama when we do..., they come into the lesson when we do practical work, like painting and stuff like that. That's when they come in. Even then Miss Langden [the drama teacher] has something to do with it, like.

Year 10 student, Lacemakers School, 18/4/91

This led to an increasing sense of the unity of the course on the part of the students, so that by Year 11 they were able to see how the coursework for the two subjects fitted together and to manage that fit for themselves.

S1: We had to be told to make a shape within the group that sort of signified a certain emotion, then we had to draw a poster or something for the emotion project.

S2: Yeah we had to do some sort of theatre design, a set, masks, costume or anything to do with emotions. Then you move on to a different project, do the drama side of that and then the theatre design. Yeah, it was all balanced out.

S3: Now we've got the detailed investigation which is picking one play or a subject, to making sets, costumes and things like that.

CP: Is that for art or the drama?

S1: Drama.

S3: It's for drama, but we can use it for art.

Year 11 students, Lacemakers School, 17/4/91

Outcomes or Experiences?

You know, we would talk about things like going on journeys, and, it sounds a bit banal, I know, but I think it's right that we're trying to develop good experiences and we're not that desperately interested in what the outcomes are.

Martin Morton, assistant deputy curriculum, Lacemakers School, 30/1/91

Connected with the debate about whether to carry out the same or parallel tasks is a variety in the degree of emphasis given to the outcomes of a piece of work in terms of assessment, and the experiences that students go through in carrying it out. For some teachers this presented a serious dilemma; it was considered to be a problem at Shipbuilders, where there was concern that the level of difficulty involved in the writing of the children's books would not be appreciated by the examination moderator.

It's a problem - and I can't, either, write a report saying although this child can't write a discursive piece very well, in discussion he has been able to - well it usually is he, too - he has been able to make very clear that he understands why he has done certain things. So there is a problem there. On the other hand it isn't a problem. I mean it's a problem if we're purely exam orientated. I think that we can also accept that as a learning experience of the child it's very valuable, and I think that sort of competence will always be there because they'll always be able to pick up on that.

Jenny Sims, English teacher, Shipbuilders School, 19/3/91

An exclusive focus on outcomes tended to lead to fragmentation and the use of parallel tasks as teachers became more interested in producing pieces that would be easy to mark than in the learning taking place on the way to these, particularly if this learning lay outside their subject area. The better integrated projects tended to be designed by teachers who gave holism priority over subject outcomes. However, the need to conform to subject-based assessment could make this hard, and could thwart otherwise holistic intentions.

I think it's great and wonderful teaching the environment in a cross curricular way, but as soon as you put an exam outcome on the end of it, you begin to destroy it...

Robert Partington, biology teacher, Lacemakers School, 4/6/91

Some teachers, nevertheless, came to an acceptable compromise. For those Lacemakers students who took design and communication, one piece of work formed their mathematics coursework. There remained problems in using it for assessment in design and communication, mainly due to widely differing coursework deadlines. However, Barry Johnson, the head of CDT, did not see this as a problem.

 So what we thought was, what we've always done in the past is, they've done their major design and communication project with the assessment for GCSE, but you wouldn't tip them into that without some prior project work, so the idea was to use this as the vehicle for that as well.

CP: The D and C project would normally be bigger than this anyway, wouldn't it?

Oh, much heavier, yeah, and it would be obviously then significantly harder from Colin's point of view to mark it as well. Much more work for him, so we thought it was better to run a mini project in design and communication which was basically, would be used in a way of teaching some of the graphic technique and the project method, and producing this project all at the same time, so that then they will be ready by, say September, to start the first bits of their design and communication major project.

Barry Johnson, Lacemakers School, 17/1/91

Resources

At Stonemasons, the students were supported in working across subjects by the development of interdisciplinary resource packs. These were collections of material that students could refer to when carrying out individual projects and were thematically based, rather than subject-centred. John Blackwell, who had largely been responsible for their development, considered that it was particularly important that they were housed centrally, in the library, so that not only could the students have access to them easily, but so could the various departments.

 I mean, as a geographer I've built one up on volcanoes and earthquakes, with things like slides and videos and newspaper articles and things on recent earthquakes and stuff, and because they're centrally housed they can be used by the English department for cross-curricular things.

John Blackwell, Stonemasons School, 25/1/91

Stonemasons was the only school that used resources in this way, and it may have been a factor in students' ability to work successfully across the curriculum without the staff doing the same.

Nothing?

In some cases I finally came to the conclusion that nothing really crossed the curriculum at all. This was when pieces of work were completed in one subject and then handed intact to another without being altered in any way. Often, indeed, even this transfer was not intended at the time the work was carried out. Such straightforward transfer of work often happened when pieces of writing completed for one subject area were also submitted for English. Donald Sidcup, the head of English at Shipbuilders, explains the sort of thing that is used:

 One boy put something in for advertising which was brilliant, absolutely brilliant. Advertising is traditionally art and then English, but we do not have the time or the language or whatever to study it in the depth that you would in media studies and this boy put in a piece of work in and he had photographs, storyboards, I think he did an advert for...[...]...a local firm. And it was absolutely brilliant, conceptually, in every sense of the word. We had a girl who did, I think for child studies, a project on playgroups...[...]...and I think somebody did something on play equipment, what was dangerous and what wasn't. So we have actually tried to cast the net wide on it, I had one boy who was going to do something in PE on heading footballs, that is his project...[...]... there was one girl who did a great piece of writing which was a description of a beach, she'd done it for geography, and it was a beach throughout the year, and that was a great piece of work.

Donald Sidcup, Shipbuilders School, 6/11/90

The head of history at Lacemakers felt that he could probably 'take in' English coursework in the same way.

 I mean I could go and chat to say the head of English and say I'm looking for a piece of coursework which fulfils this criteria, what have you got ... , oh that would be empathy, that would be such and such. When you've done them could I have a photocopy of each one and I'll mark it too or we could do the same thing and double mark it.

Paul Barker, Lacemakers School, 30/1/91

While such trading of coursework saves students time and may give them a better context for carrying out pieces of writing, it does not seem to be cross-disciplinary, inasmuch as the work is conceived of and carried out in one subject area, entering another simply as an afterthought. Most important, neither teacher nor student takes a cross-disciplinary approach to it. It is thus unlikely that it will lead to a deeper realisation of the links between subjects; that it can be dual-assessed is more likely to be seen by students as just another of the mysteries of coursework assessment.

Approaching cross-disciplinary work in this way is also likely to lead to inflexibility on the part of teachers when they come together to plan. This is particularly likely to become a problem if teachers of one subject believe that a piece of work will be useful to another, but do not discuss it with the other teachers until a relatively late stage. At Stitchers, for example, Stephen Fieldwork, the head of geography, had several ideas about where he could work with the mathematics department, but wanted to have the work completed within his subject area before he approached them.

Now that one we haven't incorporated yet with maths, I'm hoping that we can, but I want to go to Sarah with it … if you want, that completed and say there we are, now that's what we do, can you use?

Stephen Fieldwork, Stitchers School, 31/10/90

Unfortunately, for Sarah Cordingley, the head of mathematics, the way that the work was done was as important as the content covered, so that by this stage it was too late for collaboration. Stephen Fieldwork also seemed to regard such movement of work as one-way, with geography work going to mathematics and science but none coming back in. There seems again to be a desire here to 'do cross-curricular work' without actually changing subject-based practice.

Crossing the Curriculum: a multiple process?

Cross-subject work thus has many definitions and interpretations, with a resultant variety in approaches to its planning and execution. In considering who or what actually took the step across I sought to highlight this and illuminate the implications for practice. As ever, individuals' explanations of what they are doing affect what they think is possible; in approaching interdisciplinary coursework, variations in these will need to be borne in mind by curriculum innovators.

In many cases, teachers asked students to work across the curriculum in the hope that they would thereby come to a deeper realisation of the links between subjects. At the same time, however, those teachers themselves showed a reluctance to work beyond their own subject areas, with the result that the nature of such connections was not always totally clear to them, let alone to the students. In this situation it is quite likely that students will miss the point entirely, and the teachers will have put in a good deal of work to relatively little effect in terms of students' understanding of the unified nature of knowledge and their ability to transfer it between subject areas. In the case study schools, it was only those students supported in cross-subject work both by an emphasis on independent learning and by interdisciplinary resources who were able to make such links alone.

If it is only teachers who work across subject areas, they may themselves be able to develop a clearer understanding of interdisciplinary links, but are still not in a better position in terms of conveying this to students, who may be unable to appreciate why an individual teaches more than one subject. At the same time there may be worries about expertise, with teachers feeling a lack of confidence when teaching classes in subjects other than their own. The projects that worked best, in terms of being well integrated and having that integration understood by the students, were those in which both teachers and students crossed the curriculum. This was generally achieved through joint planning combined with team-teaching for at least part of the time, so that subject expertise was preserved and curricular connections were made explicit to students by the nature of the work and the way in which it was presented.

3 Agendas: Why do cross-disciplinary work?

Agendas concern the intentions, hopes and objectives that individuals, people taking particular rôles, and institutions bring to a situation. All aspects of any innovatory project are mediated and transformed by the agendas of those involved, particularly those of the teachers and students at the centre of the innovation, although these in their turn can be modified by participants' perceptions of the agendas of others, especially those of the senior management team. Previously held agendas affect how individuals become interested in cross-disciplinary work, and also play a part in the ways in which they come to take up rôles (such as TVEI co-ordinator) that place them in key positions for the introduction of this kind of curriculum development.

It is difficult for educational innovations to be assimilated by schools and teachers if their meanings are not shared (Fullan, 1991). The agendas of those involved form an important part of such shared meanings, because they are a significant factor in what Fullan refers to as the 'subjective realities' of these individuals. At the same time, however, a lot of the discussion that takes place in schools has the character of 'rhetoric exchange' (Sparkes, 1987); rather than an openness about the various agendas, there takes place a ritual exchange of publicly acceptable reasons for changing in a certain direction. For example, most people are reluctant to admit that one reason for taking part in curriculum change is that it will look good on their CV; they are more likely to talk about the important learning opportunities it will bring. However, the need to have something to show for their efforts in a comparatively short time is likely to lead to work rather different from that which might be planned if enhanced learning were all they had in mind.

In this chapter I am going to concentrate on the agendas that led teachers, students and parents to choose to work in a cross-disciplinary way. This focus on the multiplicity of reasons that the people in the particular situations studied had for taking a particular course of action is important for a number of reasons. When planning curricular innovations, those facilitating change need to be able to take participants' agendas into account as part of their subjective realities; these inform individuals' responses to suggestions that they alter their practices in some way. Marsh et al (1990) suggest that there are two major factors in teacher motivation towards change: their current level of job satisfaction and the nature of the proposed innovation, each individual having their own configuration of driving and restraining forces. However, as Weston (1979) points out, the way a situation or problem is defined can include in it an implied solution or next move; thus actors' agendas in framing the situation they are in will play a major part in how they see possible ways of moving on. This runs up against the tendency for curriculum developers to assume that if teachers agree with the actions being suggested, they are motivated by the same factors and have the same view of the initial situation. As will become clear, this is far from being the case. Most people seem to have in their heads an amalgam of conflicting and probably irresolvable desires, out of which a more or less coherent strategy will emerge.

Because of this, it is also important to realise how the agendas of participants will affect their approach to a particular project. For example, one of the intentions of the Project was to reduce the time that students spent on coursework, by making it possible for them to submit one piece of work for two or more subjects. However, humanities teachers at Lacemakers, who were already having to contend with a considerable amount of GCSE marking, understood also (possibly because this was a major issue for them) that it was expected to reduce *teacher* workload, which we in fact thought was unlikely to happen. When the introduction of integrated humanities meant that they were, on the contrary, doing even more marking, they were understandably disillusioned. They then moved away from setting dual-accreditable tasks and increasingly asked students to do different pieces of work for each subject, because these were easier to mark, thus increasing the load on students, in complete opposition to our original intentions. Such misunderstandings can occur at all levels, and may be a particular problem in situations of unequal power and control, where the more powerful party (such as the deputy head) is persuading the less powerful that an innovation will be in their interests.

Of course, not all agendas are overt and some may, indeed, be subconscious. Several people made claims about others' agendas which the latter would not necessarily admit to. Nevertheless, there was a considerable degree of candour on the part of some informants about what had brought them to cross-subject collaboration. In some cases, agendas had changed, experiences leading to an alteration in motivation. In others, covert agendas acted against stated aims and undermined the success of outcomes that an individual or group claimed to be committed to. However, even when there appeared to be a generally positive commitment to cross-disciplinary collaboration, the nature of the work developed in many cases mirrored the motivating factors behind the actors' participation in the project. These factors often had little to do with the intentions of the senior management in the school or of the Project staff; it is not therefore surprising that many of the projects did not develop as we anticipated.

Learning

Although not as frequently as we expected, some teachers were motivated to explore cross-disciplinary coursework for reasons connected with student learning. This was particularly the case at Stitchers, where learning as such was mentioned by the staff involved, particularly Stephen Fieldwork, the head of geography (who also thought that marks were improved), much more than in the other schools. Several teachers there were concerned to use cross-disciplinary work to provide a context for learning, in the hope of enhancing the transfer of knowledge between subject areas. Here, Stephen Fieldwork explains the benefits to mathematics of cross-curricular collaboration, while Darren Cashman talks about why his art input is important for geography:

 It takes theory into reality, takes theory to reality, reality back to theory and transfer of location, so they now can understand by transfer, which is the way we tend to test.

Stephen Fieldwork, Stitchers School, 31/10/90

I think that if you have that other viewpoint if you like from somebody who sees the outside world in a slightly different way ...[...]... it helps. I mean, OK it's a rock, but I think sometimes the kids benefit from actually being able to see the rock in a slightly different context of just being something which is lying around on the ground. If they can actually see some sort of appreciation of their surroundings, I mean, that all helps with the linkage of these things and it helps keep it in their minds. I think if you try and teach a kid pure information then they just forget it, if it's linked to something else it makes it that much more interesting and perhaps they tend to retain it more.

Darren Cashman, Stitchers School, 16/1/91

This interest in the use of context may reflect the nature of the project at the school; it was clear that the mathematics and science departments specifically wanted to use the geography field course to give concrete meaning to what might otherwise be fairly abstract work in their subjects. Similarly, at Lacemakers, the technology module provided a context for a piece of mathematics coursework, in the sense of giving it a purpose. The CDT teacher felt that increased transfer of knowledge between subjects was an important spin-off.

 I've always been keen to get the kids to use maths as a tool because it does bother me that some of them seem dreadfully mathematically inept when I wanted to actually use maths practically, because of course we come against it all the time, working out the area of things, how much length of metal do you need to form a loop that size or whatever, so it always shocks me how mathematically inept they are at doing that. I'm sure that if you saw them in a maths lesson they'd be quite capable of doing those calculations, it's just that they don't seem to able to see applications very easily, and I think that the liaison's been very useful.

Barry Johnson, Lacemakers School, 17/1/91

At the same school, Martin Morton, the head of art, had found that once art was combined with drama, students were much more able to build sets that one could actually act on, because they had a clearer sense of what was required. However, while this provided an additional motivation for continuing the work, it had not been a factor in its inception.

Other teachers were concerned to provide a better learning experience for students generally, in a variety of ways.

 ...that's where I'm starting from, really, I'm trying to get rid of a bit of the boredom if we possibly can and try and make it an interesting place to be.

Martin Morton, assistant deputy curriculum, Lacemakers School, 30/1/91

 The one thing that they do appreciate is that at least they can handle familiar subject matter. It is a problem in that they do have to present it in a different way, but at least there is some overlap, in that they're not handling new data or new information. It feels familiar to them. And I think that's still a great benefit.

Hilary Blondel, Head of learning support, Shipbuilders School, 4/2/91

29

Wider student experiences

Donald Sidcup, the head of English at Shipbuilders, had a wide variety of agendas in working with the children's books project. Most of these were concerned not with subject learning, but with the wider experiences of the students, as well as whole school factors, such as making the community school a reality. In one interview he gave fourteen different reasons for doing the project, mainly to do with students' personal and social development. He was particularly concerned to provide ways for boys to get involved with young children, because

our kids will all be parents one day and all of this is very valuable preparation for parenthood.

Donald Sidcup, Shipbuilders School, 6/11/90

He talked a lot about how important it was for teachers to be able to share their experiences of parenting with students who might find it hard to engage with that side of adult life.

You are also touching very very deep chords with the kids, with the teacher as parent, significant other. I mean, if I talk to the kids about something about my daughter, and I brought in her books because she was very young, only a baby. Even the roughest toughest kids were totally disarmed by her, you know, and the lads, that's very important that, for us, we found it very important that it wasn't just the girls, quite the opposite, in fact we were very interested in seeing the boys doing it. It's fascinating seeing some of the boys who are rough tough lads, one kid went in, real crew cut or whatever, all the little infants, 5 year olds, were climbing all over him because they wanted to touch his head. He was great at it.

Donald Sidcup, Shipbuilders School, 6/11/90

His remarks were echoed by other members of his department, who also felt that the project allowed them to give students experiences, such as work outside school, that would not otherwise be possible through English. They also cited the obvious interest of the students in the project as evidence that they were personally engaged with it as something more than a piece of coursework. Similarly, many students at Lacemakers thought that the combined arts course had contributed to their personal development, and some had in fact chosen it on that basis, using their experience of it in the lower school as well as advice from teachers and parents. They saw the drama side of the course as particularly important in this respect:

It's like you could use drama anywhere, like something that's been said in the lesson today, you could say to one of your mates, like, you could have and argument with them and know how to get out of it because you've been to drama, and know how to, well, like, argue back in different ways.

Year 10 student, Lacemakers School, 18/4/91

Donald Sidcup echoed this concern with the relevance of the work to 'real life' in talking about the importance of the audience of real children in the local infants' school. Not only did it make the constraints of the task (such as the use of suitable language) more meaningful to students, it also gave a clear purpose to coursework deadlines. In contrast to the normal situation in school, where the teacher is the only real audience, if a student fails to complete their book,

 You can say to the kids, well this time you are not disappointing me, you are disappointing little 5 and 6 year olds. Last time, ... it's true... I found some kids with that spur were able to put a huge amount of work in to complete the work on time. But some kids didn't and they went, and they were not very bright or sophisticated kids, and they went in to the infants school without anything. I was rather hard, in a sense on that, but then I thought, this is valuable for you, because you ought to realise that the work you are doing is significant, it is in context and there's going to be some little kid somewhere disappointed, and afterwards they'd say - I wish I had done that.

Donald Sidcup, Shipbuilders School, 6/11/90

Better Management of the Curriculum

Management of all or part of the curriculum formed a significant agenda for a range of staff at Lacemakers. Because of the modular timetable, the organisation of much of the cross-curricular work came through Peter Panther's timetable manipulations, with staff subsequently having a greater or lesser degree of choice as to whether to take part. As a result, cross-disciplinary links were often seen as being forged in fairly formal ways, and few seemed to be being developed outside this structure. This may have been because so many of the staff were involved in the initiatives already taking place that no-one had time to develop anything independently; on the other hand, it could equally be the case that in these circumstances people tend inevitably to see cross-subject work as bound up with timetable structures. Cross-subject work was generally presented to teachers as something developed through timetable manipulation; this definition of the issue may well have limited the range of people's responses to it (Weston, 1979), in the same way as Stitchers students' ideas of cross-subject work seem to have become associated totally with field work (see chapter 2). Although as time went on it became more difficult for an individual to escape being included in the cross-curricular parts of the timetable, at the time of the study it was still possible for teachers and students to opt in or out to some extent. Curriculum management at various levels was an important factor in such choices.

In setting up the modular system, and in particular the supplementary modules, Peter Panther was motivated to a considerable extent by the desire to provide for the (at that time) significant new demands of the National Curriculum, while retaining a fair degree of option choice for students. He was well aware of parental concern about reduced subject choice at 14+ and wanted to offer a wider variety than other local schools. Much of the modular timetable was geared specifically to providing this; for example, it was possible to build an integrated humanities GCSE entirely from supplementary modules and thus take double science as well as a second foreign language. He also saw the development of the modular curriculum in this way as being an opportunity for the school to try out different methods of meeting the requirements of the National Curriculum, so that they would be well prepared when it reached years 10 and 11. In this view he was joined by the acting head of CDT, Barry Johnson, for whom the mathematics/technology module served a similar purpose.

 I wanted to make sure that everybody had some CDT experience in year 10 or 11, because at that time we were expecting that was going to be what the National Curriculum required, and although we guessed we were going to have to change it I saw it if you like as a stepping stone, and so that was really one of the philosophical reasons.

Barry Johnson, Lacemakers School, 17/1/91

However, the school did not in general move towards the sort of 'audit and redistribute the work' approach to the National Curriculum that was being encouraged from several quarters at the time. While acknowledging overlap, teachers tended to see this as reinforcing concepts for students, rather than as a way of reducing the curriculum content taught by any one department. There was also a feeling that if a department was to be held responsible for any particular 'bit' of knowledge, they would need to teach it themselves.

 At the end of the day we teach them to take a maths exam, and you've got to make sure they've covered the maths that fits the exam, and there's no way we'd sort of say OK we'll not do graphs because the physics department teach them all how to intercept and project backwards.

Colin Fishbourne, mathematics teacher, Lacemakers School, 2/10/90

At the same time, the mathematics department at Lacemakers were happy to 'farm out' their major piece of coursework into the technology area, maybe because it was not being used to teach much new content, and because Colin Fishbourne was timetabled to support the technology module for one lesson a week. Indeed, there were other, non-curricular advantages:

 I mean, it's saving us time and money because it's in...to be done in a different lesson. Technology are counting it as...it counts as technology on the general hours spreadsheet, so they're getting money for it.

CP: So they're also subsidising it that way.

Which saves us forking out like tons and tons of file paper, and it's given us more time to do other things in lessons, because we've lost maths time with the timetable change.

Colin Fishbourne, Lacemakers School, 2/10/90

While preserving traditional subject boundaries in terms of the staff teaching them, cross-subject collaboration at Lacemakers did allow the provision of additional GCSE courses, and this was a significant incentive for both staff and students. Roy Saunders and Robert Partington, who put together the environment course out of geography and biology respectively, were chiefly motivated by the desire to have such a course on the timetable. Similarly, the combined arts course had originated from an interest in offering drama in the upper school; timetable constraints had meant that it was only possible to do this if it was team-taught with theatre design. Although the majority of students on this course had opted for it mainly because they liked drama, several said that this had allowed them to do two subjects that they wanted to do anyway.

I chose it because I wanted to do drama and art and something else out of the same group, but I couldn't, I had to do combined arts and then do the other one.

Year 11 student, Lacemakers School, 17/4/91

In order to provide these other courses, however, the school had to operate a particularly complex timetable and option choice system, which could itself cause difficulties. This was a particular problem for the two courses which were built up from other areas, environment and integrated humanities. In the environment course, the problems of keeping track of students that the two teachers responsible only saw for part of the two year course led to a decision not to use any dual-accredited coursework but instead to get students to complete separate projects for environment, biology and geography. This resulted in coursework overload and consequent drop-out by several students. Similar things were happening in integrated humanities, where the problems of keeping track of students' work were compounded by a large number of teachers staffing the course, and the need to keep track, for assessment purposes, of what work 'belonged' to each subject.

One of the problems that wasn't addressed was actually shaping up the criteria and where they were coming from in their different areas, and in a sense that was left until very late on. Now I think when given those criteria they tended not to be particularly open minded about what they were delivering, or where they could draw them out, and that seems to be the problem. What it wants is a nice neatly packaged and concise piece of work that they can mark very quickly. What they don't want is a rambling piece that takes a lot of picking through. And that's still a problem. And I think to a certain extent several areas have sort of side stepped by dropping in pieces of course work.

Peter Panther, deputy head, Lacemakers School, 2/7/91

In this situation, the pressures of coursework administration can make teachers reluctant to work in ways that require them to think about their subject area in more adventurous terms. For example, the art department at Lacemakers had attempted to get more involved with history coursework, but with little success.

Somebody from the art department came in, with a load of pictures, a load of sketches done by pupils, excellent work, and they asked me if that would enhance the history or could it be used for history, and I looked at a couple of drawings and I said Yeah, that could be used in history, that could be used by pupils. He said oh great. I said it's worth two marks.

Paul Barker, head of history, Lacemakers School, 30/1/91

As Peter Panther commented:

And of course the historians just weren't interested at all. They don't see it as being necessarily relevant and they were concerned with more specific things like getting the coursework out of the way in time.

Peter Panther, Lacemakers School, 2/10/90

Staff Development

The senior managements of the schools generally saw the use of cross-disciplinary work as a means to staff development. This was particularly the case at Stitchers, where the TVEI co-ordinator, who had been a key figure in establishing cross-subject links, believed that experiences outside one's own subject made for better teaching generally.

 I would hope that you would see that people that have been involved in cross-curricular teaching in this school are the more enlightened better classroom teacher. I would believe that they should be...I don't know whether that is the case, but...as you go round I think...teachers that work in narrow curriculum areas and just see their own subjects as the be all and end all of everything, I don't think are ultimately good teachers. They don't teach the whole kid and that's what we are working against.

Graham Peacock, Stitchers School, 4/12/90

This feeling that working in a cross-curricular way is personally enhancing was echoed by Martin Morton, the art teacher at Lacemakers who had worked for longest in the combined arts course. He felt that working with drama in particular had an enormous amount to offer staff:

 I actually also believe that all teachers should have to go and work in there as well, 'cause I've learned a lot about myself in there and I've learned a lot about the way I relate to kids in there, and again, that is as important, in my view, as the way in which the curriculum is shaped.

Martin Morton, Lacemakers School, 30/1/91

Others in the school were less ambitious, but still felt that the way work was done in one subject could have positive influences on another. Peter Panther, the deputy head, was particularly keen for approaches from the technology area to rub off on the mathematics department.

 If we are producing an active approach to maths coursework then I think that's a great step forward, and we need to keep chipping away at little bits of it in the same way.

Peter Panther, Lacemakers School, 17/1/91

At Stonemasons, the main motivating factors for both the deputy head, Jim Branestawm, and the TVEI co-ordinator, Gordon Swallow, were the school's comparatively poor examination results and the disparity of achievement between subjects. Their intention was to introduce cross-disciplinary work on an individual basis through the development of Flexible Learning approaches.

Looking just quickly at the exam results when I first came here, there was an obvious problem. Seaview...a secondary modern in Coastown...The grammar schools in Coastown take off 25% of the year group so it is a really big hefty chunk. The exam results at Seaview were better than they were here looking at that year, the first year, when I came, and really talking to Jim Branestawm about the possibilities and what could we do about it, I mentioned this project and he was keen to do something about that.

Gordon Swallow, Stonemasons School, 22/11/91

This was connected with another important agenda for Jim Branestawm, raising the level of staff awareness of the learning process.

When I first came here in January '88 I was concerned that teachers were traditional in their approaches to learning generally and there was not much discussion of learning in school, it just wasn't sort of a common topic. And so I was just keen to get something going along those lines.

Jim Branestawm, Stonemasons School, 13/12/90

They intended to start by developing an action research group of interested staff, who would concentrate on flexible approaches to teaching and learning. However, the staff themselves had other, prior, agendas, which in the event altered the development of the project.

When we started the staff were saying well, you know, but we haven't got the resources, so it's no good getting into this because we haven't really got the resources, so we started off on the resources.

Jim Branestawm, Stonemasons School, 13/12/90

Thus an important opportunity for staff development was delayed, due to a mismatch of agendas between teachers and senior management. This was a recurring theme throughout the work of the Project.

Subject-based Agendas

Even when a group of teachers is ostensibly working on a cross-disciplinary project, their agendas may not be focused on its cross-curricular aspects. This was especially true of the teachers working on the children's books project at Shipbuilders. Although it was considered an important and interesting piece of work, particularly by the English staff, this was from the point of view of its position as a piece of subject-based work, irrespective of the collaboration with the art department.

We actually, I don't think we actually thought about it in terms of cross-curricular work, we just thought of it in terms of being English work.

Donald Sidcup, head of English, Shipbuilders School, 6/11/90

This lack of emphasis on the cross-curricular nature of the task may have arisen because both departments were already doing a version of the project before they started to collaborate, and only realised this when the school joined the Project.

 We'd done it the year before, and that was why, we were approached by Rosemary in November, all departments were approached to see if there was any work that had been repetitive that we had done, and we targeted that as something that we had done and that we could actually do together.

Sally Brightday, head of art, Shipbuilders School, 6/11/90

The previous existence of the childrens' book project in both departments (and in child development, who continued to do it independently) may be why in practice there was so little communication between the teachers involved about the work to be carried out. For example, members of the English department decided on the timing of their work without consulting their colleagues in art and there seems to have been minimal discussion about what each syllabus required for assessment. Consequently, the liason was often left to students, who generally gave up trying to make a joint piece of work and did two separate pieces. Although several members of the English department were involved, only one, Jenny Sims, seems to have had any regular liason with Sally Brightday. It is interesting in view of this that she shifted her agenda with regard to the project over the course of the year. Having begun, like the rest of the department, by seeing it as primarily an English project, she came to the conclusion that

 This time I'm going to be doing it a bit differently because I'm going to see beforehand how much art input I can get, and possibly with child development as well. I thought I would try and see what children are doing in those two areas.

CP: So you're going to try and increase the cross-curricularity of it?

Yes, because I've found that it produced particularly good results.

Jenny Sims, Shipbuilders School, 19/3/91

Difficulties occurring because participants whose agendas were focused on one particular subject found themselves involved in a two-subject project were also in evidence among the combined arts students at Lacemakers. As I said earlier, the majority of these had chosen combined arts because it was the only way that they could do drama (art was offered alone elsewhere) and, while some of these welcomed the opportunity to study art as well, others saw it as a burden.

 I think you should skip that and go on with the drama. What's art learn you? It should be an art lesson if you want to do art, not some stupid idiot coming in and doing art with you when you're supposed to be doing drama.

Year 10 student, Lacemakers School, 18/4/91

Many of the combined arts students referred to the subject as 'drama' and one or two also claimed not to have known that it was a dual option and to have thought they were choosing drama alone. Probably as a result of this focus only on one aspect of the course, several of those in year 10 said that they could not see what the art teachers were doing in the lesson. Although the staff pointed out that this tended to resolve itself to some extent as the students started their joint coursework tasks in year 11, it is clearly difficult to teach an integrated course when the agendas of several of the students are not at all directed towards integration.

Agendas focused on teachers' own subject areas could also increase their commitment to cross-disciplinary collaboration, for a variety of reasons. Several teachers felt that working with other subjects enhanced their own area in one way or another. This was mainly in the form of opportunities to provide experiences that might otherwise not be possible. Sometimes this was because only staff from other areas had the necessary expertise.

> It's better for the kids because there's no way the maths department can offer the skills in a workshop. You see we can do all you like in three or four weeks, but we have not got the piece of paper that says you can take the kids in the workshop.

Colin Fishbourne, mathematics teacher, Lacemakers School, 17/1/91

Roy Saunders, the head of geography, was quite explicit about the importance of departmental agendas, concerning both subject status and student experiences, in the development of the environment course:

> We wanted to do this, we felt it would help *our subjects* and also give *our subjects* higher status and help them, in terms of development work, in terms of the subject areas. I mean we wanted to involve fieldwork, which was... at that particular time, I mean, you think back in two years ago the death knell was the '88 Act, and you can't charge and all this business, and fieldwork went out the window, nobody was doing any fieldwork. We certainly feel that it's a very valuable part of the curriculum, so we were saying, well, we want to get them out.

Roy Saunders, Lacemakers School, 4/6/91

This desire to use the cross-subject link to replace or make up for parts of one's own subject perceived as having been lost for various reasons was also a large part of the agenda brought to design and technology by Darren Cashman, an art teacher working as part of the new subject team at Stitchers. He anticipated that in the following year the art department would have its teaching hours cut and saw collaboration with design and technology as a way of making up some of the shortfall.

> I mean, working in technology, I see cross-curricular links if you like, as being the golden opportunity for me to actually make sure the kids are picking up what I'd like them to learn in art, in other areas, because I could teach bits and pieces, I should imagine, from almost every area in the school, but I can't do, we can't do everything, and especially not in an hour, so we'd like to see some of that time, if you like, made up within that three hours [of design and technology].

Darren Cashman, Stitchers School, 16/1/91

An agenda arising out of a teacher's own subject area could thus move projected collaboration in either direction. If collaboration as such furthers the interest of the subject or department, then there is an additional motivation to make the innovation work. However, it seems that if teachers are to adapt work that they are already doing to meet the demands of cross-disciplinary projects, they will have to be firmly convinced of the subject-based benefits if they are not to end up collaborating in name only.

Student Agendas

Student agendas can make or break a project. Quite apart from anything else, it is they who, at the end of the day, have to carry out the work, and, in doing this, to make explicit the links between the collaborating subjects. In some cases, where the relationship between the subjects had not sufficiently been thought through by the teachers, this meant that it had to be built by the students themselves in the course of their learning, with the consequent extra work this involved. At the same time, it appears that students' agendas as regards coursework, and indeed schoolwork in general, are largely instrumental (Brown, 1987; Turner, 1983). Basically, they want to get their coursework done, pass their examinations and use their qualifications for something more important. The only significant exception that I found to this was the commitment of the Lacemakers students to the combined arts course, which several said they would happily do all day, indefinitely.

A consequence of this is that whether or not teachers' agendas are focused around such things as learning, transfer of knowledge or students' wider experiences, they will still need to think in instrumental terms when planning cross-disciplinary courses, if they are to communicate successfully with the students. One of the more striking findings of the interviews with students at Stitchers, for example, was their seeming inability to think in terms of what they had learned when evaluating the success or otherwise of the cross-subject field course. The following exchange is typical:

 CP: Do you think doing the piece of joint work helps you understand the work you have done, or does it make no difference at all?

It's made it easier, because we're doing one project for two subjects, instead of having to do a geography and then coming back and doing another one for maths. So it's helped in that way.

CP: You mean its helped save time, or has it actually made it easier to do?

Yeah.

CP: In what way is that?

Because the Geography project was a long project, it took a lot of time and it was taking up...we had so many weeks on it once we come back and if we'd had a separate one for maths as well, then I don't think everyone would have got it done in time. So combining it together, it helped us as well.

Year 11 student, Stitchers School, 31/10/90

Given this emphasis on getting the work done as opposed to learning something more thoroughly, it is not surprising that students can be resistant to work that does not seem to have a clear coursework or examination outcome. Peter Panther, the deputy head at Lacemakers, was particularly aware of this problem, and it was one reason why the integrated humanities course there had been designed to incorporate work from PSE. While it was possible to put on courses simply to give a broader general education, he felt that

> The kids don't...they don't like too many modules which don't have an outcome, and if they go to a module which doesn't have an outcome they like it to be clear, and they like it to be active, and provided that happens, then it's OK.

Peter Panther, Lacemakers School, 12/11/90

This was reflected in the fourth and fifth year curriculum, which, despite the use of supplementary modules to widen students' general education, was organised so that, with the exception of the modern language and music modules, everything contributed to some GCSE somewhere. Nevertheless, this was not necessarily seen as sufficient. Subject status might also play a part, as suggested by Barry Johnson, the main contributor to the mathematics/technology module:

> I think the maths, the idea that they're actually doing something that contributes to something very important like maths is, you know, has fired a few of them up.

Barry Johnson, CDT teacher, Lacemakers School, 17/1/91

Issues of subject status also played an increasing rôle in changing student agendas as the course went on. When the Lacemakers students had chosen their options (and thus their route through the modules) in the middle of Year 9, some of them appeared to have indulged in what Peter Panther later termed 'GCSE hunting', unnoticed by the school at the time. He describes his surprise when he discovered this:

> So I said, well, you know this contributes to integrated humanities and then it all started you see. 'Oh, this is where it all fits together' and this, that and the other. This is where they started comparing, you know, 'I do combined arts *and* I'm doing .. *and* I'm doing environment .. and I'm doing .. my mam says this that and the other.' And it was really queer, I was a bit shocked actually. Yes, and they were comparing notes as to how many GCSEs they could get...
>
> :
>
> :
>
> :
>
> ...and the rest were ... were all up in arms because these kids were doing eleven, and they said, well, we didn't know that it was possible to get eleven if you did this that and the other. Which suggested that what they would have actually done was distort their option choices simply to get eleven GCSEs.

Peter Panther, Lacemakers School, 12/11/90

However, as these year 11 students came under increased pressure to complete coursework for all their GCSEs, they began to reconsider whether they really needed passes in so many subjects, and again, subject status began to play a part in their decisions. One course to suffer as a result of this was the GCSE environment, which lost several students at a fairly late stage, understandably, as far as the staff teaching it were concerned.

 ...more important I think is the fact that *they* start to realise that eight good ones is better than eleven not so good, and if it means they don't get their English and their maths at Grade Cs, well, hang on, someone will say, well you haven't got English or maths, so what you've got your environment or you've got geography or whatever, you ain't got your English and maths, and I think that's what they began to appreciate.

Roy Saunders, head of geography, Lacemakers School, 4/6/91

Parental Agendas

It is school perceptions of parental agendas, more than those agendas themselves, that are relevant here. These were a significant factor in the developments at Lacemakers, where it was felt that GCSE hunting stemmed from parental ambition as much as from the students themselves.

 Parents ask all sorts of questions about it but the only question they're really interested in is the answer to, how many GCSEs do they get? It's true!...You know, I mean, it's cynical, but it's true, and so when you're actually discussing, you say, well, of course they all get an extra GCSE out of it - at least one extra GCSE; they can get two, or three, and then their eyes light up.

Peter Panther, Lacemakers School, 2/10/90

It was also found at Lacemakers that parents were able to manipulate the modular option choice system to an extent that had not really been anticipated. One of the underlying reasons for building the integrated humanities GCSE out of a combination of 'mainline' and supplementary modules of the separate subjects was to ensure that no student completely gave up either history or geography before the end of year 11. Thus the school's intention was that most students would still take one humanities subject, supplemented by a module of the other, with the integrated humanities qualification as an incentive to take this seriously. They found, however, that

 the takeup in individual humanities subjects from the good scientists and mathematicians has dropped, because they say, well, because with integrated humanities you don't need to do it, do you, we've got a balance, haven't we, because we've got it all back here.

Peter Panther, Lacemakers School, 12/11/90

Seeing the humanities subjects as less academic, some parents wanted to take this opportunity to opt for two modern foreign languages as well as double science. Having promoted the system as ensuring a broad curriculum, Peter Panther then had to live with the consequences:

We are talking about very well informed parents who had actually done their homework and, you know, I am saying that this is a safety net to keep a balance in the curriculum. And they're saying, we want to use your safety net, we want to jump on it, right, and what do you say, you're going to take it away? and I say, no, no. Fine, you know, OK.

Peter Panther, Lacemakers School, 12/11/90

In a system such as that operating at Lacemakers, where initial option choice can have a significant influence on the degree to which students take part in cross-disciplinary projects, parental agendas can thus be a distorting force acting at a tangent to the school's intentions. It thus becomes even more important for it to be made clear to parents and students what potential consequences, such as later coursework overload, need to be taken into account when making such decisions.

Other factors

 You don't like to say no.

Robert Partington, biology teacher, Lacemakers School, 4/6/91

Several teachers were not particularly committed to cross-disciplinary work, but did it because they were asked to, or generally felt that it was expected of them. This was particularly the case at Lacemakers, due to its being built into the timetable, but happened in all the schools to a greater or lesser extent. Pressure to offer something to the Project team so that we would work with the school (part of a wider agenda concerned with being part of a national project) could be an additional factor in this. When I first visited Shipbuilders, Rosemary Benbridge, who co-ordinated the Project in the school, got the (mistaken) impression that we were insisting on two projects in each school.

 You wanted two definite projects so I sort of plucked up my courage and said, well, you know, I'll see what I can do with the CPVE group and that...we said, OK, that's fine, we've got English and art, and this one, but I did it, I must confess, with a bit of a heavy heart because I didn't know whether I could do anything and, you know, I wasn't sure it was going to be successful.'

Rosemary Benbridge, Shipbuilders School, 15/10/90

However, even though a teacher might feel under pressure to carry out an innovative project, other factors might play a part.

 And I thought it would be something interesting for me to teach.

Robert Partington, Lacemakers School, 4/6/91

However, expressions of interest in the work tended to come from a focus on the subject base, rather than a specific leaning towards cross-disciplinary issues. Teachers were often attracted to a piece of work because they thought it would bring out the best in their subject, and became more reluctant when the need to make compromises in order to collaborate effectively threatened their normal ways of working.

Other, more micropolitical, factors played a part in decisions to become involved in cross-subject projects. Particularly in schools where TVEI had a high profile, it was an important area to be seen to be working in. Fullan (1991) points out that there is a tendency for people to adopt any innovation as a means to personal advancement; this can lead to ill-thought out or inappropriate projects or to disillusionment if the resulting career developments fail to materialise (Weston, 1979). At Stitchers, several of the key actors were middle managers keen for promotion. There was an underlying feeling on the part of some teachers that others they were working with were mainly interested in extending their empire. In particular, the rôle of school co-ordinator for the Project (which was basically an organisational job, involving liaison between staff and with myself) became quite hotly contested at one point, with both the head of science and another member of his department demanding to know why the name of Sarah Cordingley, the head of mathematics, was 'getting bandied about here, there and everywhere', as the Project co-ordinator, when other people were also involved in such work (field notes, 16/1/91). At the same school, Stephen Fieldwork, the head of geography, expressed the frustration that came with working with people whose main interest in collaboration (he felt) was their own promotion:

> They say, 'we do the Romans,' but what's really happening is they're all doing their own thing. That's not cross-curricular at all. They just say, 'we do the Romans' so that some plonker can put it on his CV and say, 'I introduced this'.

Stephen Fieldwork, Stitchers School, 27/9/90 (field notes)

At Lacemakers, Peter Panther felt that he could detect empire building of a similar sort on the part of whole departments, both in the writing of supplementary modules and in moving towards the cross-curricular provision in year 7:

> And they see the same situation there, in that, you know, 'Here's a hole in the curriculum. Let's lay claim to it.'

Peter Panther, Lacemakers School, 2/10/90

While cross-subject work continues to be promoted through TVEI and the SCAA, it is likely that ambitious teachers will, for better or worse, jump on its bandwagon. And there is another side to this coin, as explained by the head of humanities at Lacemakers. Although he co-ordinated the integrated humanities GCSE, he was not wholeheartedly behind it, and felt that it was low priority for the students. However, he had poignantly powerful reasons for continuing to struggle with the administrative difficulties:

> To offset that I have to think of people's jobs, because, maybe I shouldn't even be saying this to you, but obviously you are aware that in Fordingshire, as in most counties, cutbacks are the order of the day, and if this does protect a colleague's job, then I've got this sort of dichotomy that, is a course really worth while? Well, if it keeps old so and so in a job, because he's only doing 20% of his timetable in this, then it's worth doing because he's a good teacher; which is a hell of way to run an education organisation.

Paul Barker, head of history, Lacemakers School, 30/1/91.

Summary: a Multiplicity of Agendas

It is clear from the foregoing analysis that teachers and students bring a multiplicity of agendas to cross-disciplinary innovation. Some of these are to do with learning, and include a concern with the cross-subject transfer of knowledge, often through the contextualisation of knowledge 'belonging' to one subject within the pedagogy of another. Teachers may want to provide a context or purpose for the learning of otherwise abstract knowledge, or to give students continuity of content to be dealt with in a variety of subject-based ways. There was a concern to make learning more interesting for students and to improve their experience of school in general. Some teachers also expressed an interest in the personal development of students and in the potential for cross-disciplinary collaboration to make possible experiences that might otherwise have been difficult to provide, such as work out of school or with younger children. This was particularly so among those who stressed the relevance of what they were doing to 'real life'.

The potential for better curriculum management also played a part in the decision to commence cross-subject work, especially among senior and middle managers. At a time when the Year 10 and 11 curriculum looked as if it was going to be very crowded and nationally uniform, there was a hope that it would be possible to continue providing some choice alongside National Curriculum entitlement. Time and money were at a premium, so anything that would save these for a department was to be welcomed; this could be an important trade-off in the loss of total control over the teaching of one's subject. Other subject-based agendas also played a part, several teachers mainly being motivated by intra-subject considerations, the cross-curricular element being of lesser importance. Such agendas might include the project's relevance to their subject area, the possibility of giving students access to experiences within the subject (such as practical work) that the department could not provide alone, or improving the general profile of the subject in the school.

Several people claimed that working in a cross-disciplinary way made for better teachers, less bound up in their own subject cultures and more concerned with 'teaching the whole child' than imparting discrete bits of knowledge. This occurred because staff found themselves exposed to alternative ways of working, which might lead to them developing their own practice or just generally thinking about learning more than before. The encouragement of active learning in various parts of the school was a concern of several senior managers. The development of different sorts of resources for learning might also play a part in this.

Students and parents generally had much more instrumental agendas than teachers. They had a particular concern with outcomes, in the form both of a large number of GCSE passes and of good grades in higher status subjects. This latter had considerable influence on decisions to drop or cease working for subjects that were considered less important, as well as on option choice. Because of this, it was felt by teachers that it was important for work to have a clear GCSE outcome, rather than being presented as part of a broad general education. Students, who were often under time pressures with a lot of pieces of work to complete, were often more concerned with getting the work done than with what they learned from it.

Finally, a number of miscellaneous and at times idiosyncratic agendas also played their part. Being part of a national project had been a factor in the taking on of a cross-curricular commitment in some cases, as had the feeling that taking part in such innovations was generally expected. Desire for promotion also featured, as did personal and departmental empire-building and a concern to protect departmental jobs. On the other hand, some teachers became involved at least partly out of personal interest in the work itself or in the idea of working outside their own subject area.

Working with Multiple Agendas

 The incentives for schools to plan cross-curricular approaches to mathematics are clear:

- they reflect the real world in which we live;
- they enable more efficient use of time to be planned for;
- the contribution of mathematics to other areas of the curriculum can be maximised;
- working in a variety of contexts helps pupils to learn

(National Curriculum Council, 1989a, pages F1-F2)

 The co-ordinated planning made possible by cross-referencing between core curriculum subjects will reduce repetition and overlap in both the planning and delivery of the curriculum and in assessment of its outcomes. This will be a significant factor in helping teachers and schools move towards a more efficient use of curriculum time.

(National Curriculum Council, 1989b, page C8)

Although most of the teachers in the study would happily acquiesce with the statements from the NCC quoted above, one of the more striking findings of the case study interviews was how comparatively few of them volunteered efficient organisation of the curriculum or enhancement of learning as reasons for working in a cross-disciplinary way. While such agendas had their place, this was only as one or two in a much wider range of factors. In entering and continuing with the process of collaborating with someone from another subject department, teachers tend to weigh up a multiplicity of reasons for and against, many of which have little to do with learning at all. Furthermore, while it is true that some senior managers hoped in the early days of the National Curriculum that curriculum overload could be reduced by an increase in interdisciplinary links, this has had a comparatively unimportant rôle in the motivation of individual teachers.

A major agenda of the people who initially set up the Project was to encourage schools to work with real problems, conjoined with a belief that real problems require cross-curricular solutions, and that consequently such links should be developed in schools. However, such beliefs were not mentioned by any of those actually doing cross-subject work, with the exception of Martin Morton, the art teacher at Lacemakers, who thought that his students' experience with drama made them better able to understand the issues and constraints involved in set design. This may explain why so few of the projects carried out in the schools involved 'real world' issues and why, where such problems were tackled, they were often shorn of their original complex constraints (for example, some Lacemakers' technology projects were about designing an adventure playground for the local park; no consideration was made of the fact that the park was already fully used and that another facility would have to be removed if this were actually to be built). In retrospect, I feel that, because they were interested in our proposed solution, interdisciplinary work, we tended to assume that those working in the schools shared our agendas. The evidence of the case study is that, by and large, this was not the case.

This may be connected with the high but vaguely defined profile of cross-disciplinary work at the time of the research. During this period the NCC published documents relating to cross-curricular themes, and there was mention of cross-subject collaboration in most National Curriculum documents, as well as in GCSE examination syllabuses. Consequently, there was a general feeling in schools that cross-curricular work was a good thing, although it was not often entirely clear why. There has been a lack of precision in writing about interdisciplinary approaches, with statements of purpose being particularly unclearly presented, maybe because of a failure to recognise the multiplicity of agendas involved. As Gordon Swallow remarked about a colleague's proposed M.A. dissertation:

 I can imagine someone writing a thesis on cross curricular issues - it's just like trying to catch the fog.

Gordon Swallow, TVEI co-ordinator, Stonemasons School, 22/11/90

At the same time there has been very little written about the reality of cross-disciplinary work. Much is said about what should happen, too little about what actually does. This ignores the complex factors involved in implementation and has led to a simplistic approach on the part of curriculum developers, including ourselves.

The main difficulty in working with multiple agendas is the tendency for people to behave as if such multiplicity did not exist. However, unless the complexities of actors' motivations are recognised, misunderstandings and consequent resentments will continue to occur. Such misunderstandings stem from the tendency for individuals and groups to frame their interpretations of situations in terms of their agendas, and thus to conceive of possibilities for action in these terms. Only an awareness of the many and varied agendas that can be brought to a situation will make it possible to take account of the intentions and hopes of all the actors involved. If this is ignored, it is likely that any innovation will be fraught with difficulty and conflict.

4 Decisions

 ...we must consider decision-making theories as part of a value commitment to liberal democracy. There is a belief that individuals should assume responsibility for decision-making in institutions that affect their lives on a day-to-day basis. This commitment to decision-making has two different but related emphases: to obtain a more equitable allocation of goods, services, and knowledge; and to involve individuals in public affairs as a means of maintaining the vitality and creativity of a society. Democracy is to provide concrete forms for individual growth and self-development.

Once said, however, we are left with little to understand the nature and interest of the decision-making process. Decision-making focuses upon the surface aspects of choices made in organizations. It does not consider that many of the wants, values, and priorities of 'decision-making' are determined by the structural and historical conditions of our institutions. Certain values and rules are taken for granted, becoming background assumptions which orient participants towards definitions of problems and ways of 'thinking'

(Popkewitz, 1984, pages 173-4)

It would appear unproblematic to assume that where a school or group of teachers has begun work on a curriculum innovation, at some stage they will have taken a decision to do so. This seemed particularly clear in the case of the Project, because schools had to take a definite step in agreeing or asking to join. Given this assumption, my original intentions in enquiring into the decision-making process were to locate it within the overall time-frame of the planned work and to gain some impression of the seniority of those taking decisions, in order to see if these had any effect on the durability of projects. I was also initially more interested in the agendas and perceptions informing decisions than the decisions themselves. However, I found once I started interviewing that it could be difficult to locate such decisions at all; often, no-one would admit to having taken them. People seemed to want either to attribute decision-making to others or to present the development of the work as if it had emerged seamlessly from previous practice. I therefore began to track people's accounts of decisions more systematically, and to interest myself increasingly in a different set of questions, namely: What decisions were taken? By whom? Is this acknowledged? And what were the consequences in terms of their actions? It is these that this chapter attempts to address.

Decisions are taken at a number of levels (Smith and Keith, 1971). In the schools studied, these went broadly from the individual outwards through the department, senior management and the head, to those external to the school, such as National Curriculum working parties. At Lacemakers, the senior management had attempted to reorganise the school at an early stage to reflect the original form of the National Curriculum. The repeated changes in this led to successive re-thinking and in many ways resulted in some decisions effectively being located outside the school, particularly as questions of curriculum were often framed in terms of National Curriculum delivery, so that changing national frameworks led to changes in thinking within the institution. At the same time, these external changes also altered the range of decisions possible, particularly as there was a national move towards increased flexibility at Key Stage 4. In the main, however, I was concerned with internal decision making, both institutional and personal, and I shall concentrate on this in the discussion that follows, though it should be borne in mind that external factors, such as events in the LEA, will impinge on these processes.

Underlying this analysis is Weston's (1979) suggestion that the way in which a problem is framed can determine to a large extent what decisions can be made regarding it. She illustrates this by tracing the adoption and subsequent abandonment of an integrated science scheme in one school:

 If the 'problem' was fairly obvious - what science curriculum should be provided in the new school? - the decisive work of definition seems to have been carried out by the headmaster, and then put to the science staff: that what was needed for the new school was an integrated science curriculum. What gave this definition force is that it was accompanied by a *proposal:* that a 'ready made' course which met the needs of the school was already available. Once the definition had been accepted, then the proposal made sense; in these circumstances there was little need for the refining of the definition that takes place as proposals are suggested, 'tried out' in discussion, revised or rejected.

(Weston, 1979, page 233)

Because the problem came to the science staff already framed, the decisions that they were able to make were in effect limited by this.

We can see decision making as taking place within a 'decision field' representing the widest possible view of the area within which the decision is to be made. In Weston's case, this was the need to provide a science curriculum for the new school. There then takes place an overlapping but basically sequential process of problem framing, leading to issue definition and the formulation of proposals. As each stage is more focused than the one before, the area of the 'decision field' becomes correspondingly smaller, so that the possible range of outcomes is limited by the decision-making process. If teachers are presented with problems already framed or issues already defined, it is difficult for them to do anything except operate within this reduced decision field. To move in the opposite direction and re-pose problems (Brown and Walter, 1983), thus widening the decision field again, involves both a leap into the unknown and considerable time for open discussion. However, only by a thorough examination of a wide range of the questions that can be asked of a particular situation can the participants in a decision making process ensure that they are not following a course made obvious only by the way that the problem is set up in the first place.

In framing problems and defining issues in advance of consultation, most managers act in such a way as to control the decision making process. This is not generally a machiavellian strategy; it is easier to present an even partly-formulated problem than to describe a situation and ask people to pose for themselves the problems arising out of it. Given the timescales of most school-based decisions, it is in any case probably not feasible to do this. At the same time, by presenting teachers with decisions regarding issues that have been defined in advance by the very act of presentation, senior managers are able to delegate decisions safely; there is little likelihood that they will stray outside the expected parameters. Thus all concerned feel that authority has been shared, and managers still get something they can live with. In attempting to unpack exactly what decisions are made explicitly and what implicitly (through the action of problem framing) I hope to be able to illuminate the micropolitical forces at work here.

Ownership

 The idea of 'ownership' quickly became a key term in the new language of change. It inspired 'collective confidence' (Fullan, 1982, page 295); it made people feel that they were participating in worthwhile communal action.

(Ruddock, 1991, page 123)

One of the reasons for my difficulties in tracing decisions seems to be the reluctance of individuals to 'own' them. This is connected with a distinction between decision making and decision taking.

 Which decision-making process is chosen will largely depend on the purpose of the particular group. If its purpose is to advise the head, then the head will take the decision even if the group helps him or her to make it.

(Handy and Aitken, 1986, page 68)

Decision *making* is the process gone through in moving towards the taking of a decision; it is the (conscious or unconscious) process of problem framing, issue definition and proposal formulation. Once this has happened, a decision can be *taken*. The *taking* of a decision implies an assumption of the authority to do so and a willingness to take responsibility for the consequences; it may be more comfortable to disown the taking of the decision and therefore the associated risk. Teachers who do not feel that they have the necessary authority may believe that certain decisions are not theirs to take, despite efforts on the part of senior management to introduce at least a degree of collective responsibility by including staff in the decision *making* process. It is also possible that an individual will own or disown the same decision at different times according to the degree of risk that such ownership involves (Handy and Aitken, 1986; Fullan, 1991).

The inability to acknowledge what seemed to me a straightforward instance of a decision having been taken first came to my attention through the head of mathematics at Stitchers, Sarah Cordingley. Cross-disciplinary collaboration had started there with a group of staff being taken out of school for a day to work together. Sarah had been one of these, and indeed was involved with all the projects subsequently set up. She was interested in finding out how they had been chosen to take part and asked me several times if I could do this for her. However, when I interviewed Graham Peacock, who had set up the day, he painted a very different picture of how these individuals got involved:

 I was very much looking at home ec[6], that was one area I wanted definitely - and maths, because Sarah had made it clear that she would like to work with other departments. So what we did, I think, I can't remember this clearly, but we...I think I went public in some meeting or something like that and said this was a possibility; would any departments who were interested contact me, and I got the responses from science, geography, maths, home ec, textiles...

Graham Peacock, TVEI co-ordinator, Stitchers School, 4/12/90

---

[6] Home economics

Although Sarah seemed unwilling to take responsibility for choosing to work cross-curricularly, this decision was nevertheless acknowledged by others in the school, such as Graham Peacock. Reluctance to own one's decisions can be a two-edged sword; while it absolves one from the risk of responsibility for failure, it also means that one's successes may go unrecognised. This seemed to be the case with John Blackwell, who had had a key rôle in the development of Flexible Learning at Stonemasons, according to the TVEI co-ordinator, Gordon Swallow, and the deputy head, Jim Branestawm. Although the two men who had worked most closely with him were able to recognise his contribution, it was not appreciated by the head, who saw others who had had less input as being more centrally involved. This may have been connected with the generally self-effacing way that John tended to talk about his work.

 I first got involved with it when there was a course basically and a couple of us went along to this, we were asked to go along to this particular course, we didn't actually volunteer for it, we were just asked,...[...]...it was a course on supported self study, and it sort of grew from there really.

John Blackwell, geography teacher, Stonemasons School, 25/1/91

This growth continued until he was one of the most experienced classroom practitioners of Flexible Learning in the school and had a central rôle in the induction of others.

For a teacher not particularly interested in promotion, such self-effacement might not matter. However, Ball (1987) points out that 'acceptance of innovation decisions was found to be positively related to the degree of participation in the decision by members of the collectivity' (page 30). Teachers are more likely to be committed to an innovation if they are able to recognise their contribution to its inception. Peter Panther, the deputy head at Lacemakers, hinted at something like this when reviewing which projects had retained their initial impetus.

 Some of the things we've done are, sort of, naturally successful, almost, well that's my theory. I mean the art and combined arts business, and some of the other bits and pieces seem to be okay, they've taken root and they're developing, really.

CP: What do you mean by 'naturally successful'?

I think there was a natural commitment of the people who are responsible for it, to do it that way. We aren't asking them to do anything that they don't, that isn't somewhere pretty high on their list of priorities. I think that's important.

Peter Panther, Lacemakers School, 2/7/91

The other side of this is that it is likely that an inability to 'own' one's innovatory decisions may lead to problems in fully accepting them. Again, there may be a reluctance to take responsibility for the risks as well as the successes; where the likelihood of failure is great, this may be a sensible strategy for personal survival. Weston points out that there can be a reluctance to be responsible for 'negative' decisions, to the extent of allowing them to be taken by default, as in the case of the abandonment of integrated science by the department she studied:

Once the 'shelter' of departmental commitment had been removed, no decisive knockout blow was required to destroy the innovation; it was simply counted out. It would be in keeping with the evidence to suggest that there was an important element of laissez-faire about this episode of decision-making, so that the decision *against* integrated science in the end almost took itself. In this way no one had to carry the opprobrium for killing off the innovation, while everyone had been consulted and could be said to support the decision, even if reluctantly.

(Weston, 1979, page 255)

Handy likewise points out that two processes by which people reach decisions, 'decision by minority' and 'decision by no response'

 happen by mistake. Ideas are dropped because no-one says anything (no response) or because a few feel deeply opposed (minority). Good ideas can disappear down these plugholes if the group does not make a more determined choice of procedure.

(Handy and Aitken, 1986, page 68)

At the same time, some teachers seem (at least at times) to want to detach themselves entirely from the decision making process, and to see themselves as co-operative realisers of other people's plans. Paul Barker, the head of humanities at Lacemakers, took this line regarding the integrated humanities GCSE, which had not been his idea and about which he was rather sceptical. He seemed to prefer to have curriculum decisions taken by others and to spend his and his department's time getting on with carrying them out rather than discussing what was to be done.

 I said, let's sit down and get it done, because you could spend the rest of your life arguing about whether you should do something. Maybe I've just got this sort of, I don't know, pragmatic streak, or whatever it is, and think, that has got to be done, right, let's get it done...[...]... I can't go in to my people and say, hey look we've got this wonderful idea, because they just say, oh Paul, you know, sod off, but if I go in and say, look, we've got to do this, somebody will say, right, I'll do that bit and I'll do that bit.

Paul Barker, Lacemakers School, 30/1/91

It is unclear whether Paul's attitude is due to an impatience with abstract planning and a preference for pragmatics, or to a reluctance to take responsibility for an innovation that he did not fully support. Whatever is the case, as the administrative problems of the course became more apparent, he did take the initiative in sorting these out, partly because he could see that the blame would fall on him anyway if things continued to go wrong.

 Well it was organised mainly by Peter Panther and Martin Morton, as far as it was organised by anybody. I then realised that it has this humanities tag to it and eventually when they were looking for a whipping boy they would be looking for somebody, and I came back last, was it last September or the September before? I can't remember. Anyway, I came back and I saw Peter about it, 'I think you've got problems with it,' because nobody knew what [work] existed, and I started drawing up a system to be able to monitor it.

Paul Barker, Lacemakers School, 30/1/91

In this case, Paul Barker saw himself as rescuing the senior management team (and himself) from the consequences of earlier decisions whose implications had not been thought through. His attempts to dissociate himself from curriculum decision-making also reflect his belief that the real decisions have already been both made and taken by senior management. This is often the case in schools, where there is a tendency for 'pseudo-participation' (Ball, 1987) to predominate over genuinely equal contributions to decision making. At the same time it is often hard in the to and fro of meetings for individuals to be clear about what decision has emerged; partly due to confusion and partly to wishful thinking, people may go away with different versions of what has been agreed[7]. The decision takers may thus believe that their actions are based on a group decision-making process and be surprised when their perceptions are not shared by others,

 What's happened is that we have done the negotiations...we have negotiated it, for ... we must have been talking about this two years ago, eighteen month ago, and this has come in, and we tried it out on key people and heads of department, and as far as we were concerned there was an open discussion process. So we decided to do it ...[...]...and we produced a sort of printed sheet and a schpiel that went with it, and I was asked 'when are we going to do this?' and I said well, in September, and all of a sudden everybody started paying attention. People said well, you never asked us, when did we decide we were going to do it, we talked about it, what is going off? And all hell broke loose for maybe a fortnight.

Peter Panther, deputy head, Lacemakers School, 12/11/90

This may again be connected with a reluctance or inability on the part of some of those concerned to deal with decisions about ideas presented in the abstract. Objections may only surface when implementation begins, as some people will only then be able to see what the decision entailed.

It may be that some senior managers find it as hard as their junior colleagues to own their decisions, wanting to create a climate of collective responsibility in the face of staff resistance. An awareness that innovation is likely to be more successful if it originates from below may also lead to a degree of stage-management of this, so that a decision may be made to appear to be located at a different level to its original source.

 The idea was that we were going to present a means of working as a response to a felt need ... no, 'felt need' is a bit optimistic ... I think we actually meant to create that feeling.

CP: Who was it felt by?

It was felt by me and uh ... initially it was myself, Gordon and the previous head really.

Jim Branestawm, deputy head, Stonemasons School, 13/12/90

In suggesting a response to a 'felt need' that he intended to create, Jim Branestawm was also defining the problem as he saw it in such a way that the move to Flexible Learning methods for carrying out coursework would be the logical solution. The staff would be able to take and own this decision, but the framework within which it had been made would have been his, not theirs. This leads

---

[7] I am grateful to Paul Black for this observation

us to the consideration of what decisions people actually take, and how these are constrained by the frameworks in which they are presented.

What Decision?

 I mean, I'm sure they would argue and say that it was discussed, but it depends on what your point for starting the discussion is.

Paul Barker, head of humanities, Lacemakers School, 30/1/91

In looking at responsibility for curriculum decisions, it is necessary not only to consider who took the decision but also what exactly they decided. Decision-making in schools often takes place in stages, each decision framing the issue to be addressed at the next level down. How much genuine authority is given to individuals in determining the outcome of a particular discussion depends, as Paul Barker points out, on what your point for starting the discussion is.

At Lacemakers, decisions seemed to come in paired stages. Those about the curriculum structure generally emanated from Peter Panther's office, after discussion with his assistant, Martin Morton, and, where necessary, the head. These decisions would be in the form of proposals that could be assented to or rejected; the two of them tended to decide what they wanted to happen and then negotiated that with the rest of the staff.

 You know, those two people go in that room and talk strange things for a long time and emerge with ideas, and we get people and corner them and sort of say, how about doing this? and they say all right, or no, or do I have to, or whatever.

Martin Morton, Lacemakers School, 30/1/91

In consequence, as Martin himself recognised, little exploratory thinking about the general nature of the curriculum was done by others; proposals rather than issues were put to the staff. A certain amount of bargaining took place; for example, the mathematics department were encouraged to co-operate with the setting up of the mathematics/technology module by the extra teaching time this would give them (because they would not have to carry out a major piece of coursework in mathematics lessons). Nevertheless, Colin Fishbourne remained of the opinion that

 we were really basically pushed into doing it 'cos they wanted to do entitlement technology and no-one could think of what to do in entitlement technology and Peter said to Bill, "Would you like to run an OET[8] in technology?" and Bill, said "Oh I could consider doing that" and the next thing we knew it's on the timetable.[9]

Colin Fishbourne, mathematics teacher, Lacemakers School, 2/10/90

---

[8] open-ended task, required by the SMP mathematics GCSE

[9] I was present during some of these discussions. My own impression was that after a day of wrangling, Peter Panther and Bill Bailey negotiated a mutually advantageous deal.

However, once this agreement (under whatever degree of pressure) had been reached, the two departments were left more or less to themselves to negotiate the details of their collaboration.

Peter Panther tended to be quite explicit in his framing of what staff were able to decide; he openly put limits on what was to be negotiated. For example, in the Year 7 cross-curricular provision,

We do have constraints on it. We have said for a start it has to deliver the PSE programme and the Fordingshire agreed religious education programme.

Peter Panther, Lacemakers School, 12/1/90

This framing was at its tightest in the initial negotiations about the integrated humanities GCSE, where Paul Barker felt that the departments concerned were asked 'can you do this?' rather than 'is this a good idea?' (30/1/91). By the time the course was discussed with the humanities staff, it had already been decided that it would be based on the theme of the local environment, and so their task was framed in these comparatively narrow terms. This led to some animosity.

We were asked if we could write a module based on the local environment, which we could do, and which we did.

CP: A history based module?

A history based module, yeah. I mean, I'm talking now as head of history. ...[...]...Anyway, we produced this module, we run off the resources etc. and that was it. We subsequently found that in fact to meet the criteria we didn't actually need to produce a complete new module, if they hadn't insisted the whole thing had to be based on a local environment, because the main line historians, their piece of coursework relates to medicine, it's drawn from the *Medicine Through Time* bit, so I mean that's, well I suppose if you stretch a point you could say that it relates to the local environment, but there's no mention of the local environment there. So that actually produced a little bit of antagonism.

CP: You mean because you could have used *Medicine Through Time*?

Because we could have done it and saved ourselves a lot of work, yeah.

Paul Barker, head of humanities, Lacemakers School, 30/1/91

The historians were thus left feeling that they were effectively prevented from making the sort of curriculum decisions that they were best equipped to deal with. Freedom within constraints had been taken to the stage where those constrained had very little sense of that freedom.

Interfaces Between Decisions and Actions

Delays

There were signs from the very start of the Project that the relationship between decision and action would be an issue. In recruiting schools, we asked that they be already working on cross-disciplinary issues, and thus ready to move rapidly to designing dual accredited GCSE work. Thus it might be assumed that there was someone in the school at a moderately senior level who believed this to be the case[10]. However, when I started visiting these schools, it became clear that in many cases they might better be described as 'thinking about it'. Decisions to become involved in cross-subject collaboration had often been taken, but nothing had actually been started.

There seem to be two broad issues in this gap between decision and action. The first concerns time and opportunity. In general, schools often needed to have a pause between initially deciding to carry out cross-curricular work and the start of its implementation; staff appeared to need time to let the ideas sink in before getting down to practicalities. This appears to be a normal feature in the introduction of innovations; as Fullan points out, 'any significant innovation, if it is to result in change, requires individual implementers to work out their own meaning' (Fullan, 1991, page 106). This takes time. In some cases, a further catalysing event might be needed, such as my own first visit or the setting up of a local support group. In others, an individual might become interested but be prevented from getting further involved because of other considerations. Gordon Swallow, the TVEI co-ordinator at Stonemasons, outlines the multiple factors that operated in his case:

What, really where it started, was, I had...well going back even further than that. When I was head of Science at Goodward I read about the SITE project.

CP: So how long ago was that?

Uh, four years ago? Must be four years ago and I thought that sounded quite interesting, and the article was written by Robin Murray[11]. So I wrote to Robin Murray, because at that time I had also been made head of science and technology faculty and I saw it as a way of bringing science and technology together...[...]...it was in the very early stages of that. And he said, basically, then that he was interested in moving it out a little bit. I think there was some contact at that time with Stitchers already and [another local school]. They were involved in this sort of science technology sort of overlap and he said that he was quite interested in the possibility of moving into Camberside, but because of my, sort of, position I couldn't really get anything to happen in Camberside as such.

Then Tom Langden came to Camberside from Amberswell, as advisory teacher and I met him. I mentioned it to him, he knew about it and he then had the clout to get involved...[He set up a support group to discuss cross-curricular work]...It really started to sort of develop then, but I think that was only about two terms really. It was a very short period of time, it certainly wasn't a year. Then the SITE project had more or less finished. There had been, like, the interest created, and it must have been Tom I think who found out about your side of the project and it seemed a natural progression with the people involved to extend it into that. So that's really how I got involved.

Also, no... probably about a term later, was when I came here, my job here is looking at fourth and fifth year curriculum basically.

Gordon Swallow, Stonemasons School, 22/11/90

---

[10] Although it is possible that one or two schools in the wider study had an eye more to publicity than to participation, in the four case-study schools there does seem to have been a genuine belief that such work was already being or was about to be carried out.

[11] Project Officer for SITE (Science Into Technology Education) and co-director of the present project.

It was only at this point that he felt that he had both the authority and the support to be able to initiate cross-disciplinary coursework discussions.

Pathologies

 For the schools' purposes, verbal adoption of innovations may be entirely sufficient.

Pincus, J. 1974, Incentives for Innovation in Public Schools, Review of Educational Research, 44, 113-44 page 125, quoted in Fullan (1991) page 28

Although it took a number of years, Gordon Swallow's progress from interest to action was continuous and, ultimately, fruitful. In other cases, however, decisions seem almost to replace actions in people's heads. It is as if by taking decisions individuals come to believe that they have carried out the action it implies. The clearest example of this tendency was Simon Hastings, the media studies teacher at Shipbuilders. The first time I met him he told me that he was working on a cross-curricular module with dance (field notes, 6/11/90); however, when I interviewed him subsequently it appeared that things had not quite got to that stage.

 You see I can't actually think about doing something about dance unless I have access to Tina and the PE department and her scheme of work, ... and I see her about once a term.

Simon Hastings, Shipbuilders School, 10/1/91

Indeed, as far as I could tell, the dance teacher had not been approached at all!

It is not clear why Simon gave me two such diverse accounts at our two meetings. It may be that he was initially trying to impress me and then later felt guilty that his plans had not come to fruition. On the other hand, he was described by others in the school as someone who was very enthusiastic but difficult to pin down to specifics (field notes, 15/10/90). Simon certainly seemed to feel that he had a lot of ideas which were frustrated by adverse circumstances.

The substitution of decision for action also seemed to be a factor in the failure of the majority of the English department at this school to actually work with the art staff on what they still regarded as a joint project. Again it seemed as if a declaration (in this case to the students) that they were working with art would be enough to make the collaboration happen. Only Jenny Sims, who did discuss her work with the art staff, seemed to be an exception to this, the others leaving it up to students to bridge the gap between the two subjects. For example, when I asked Meagan Scanlan, after the project had already started, if she had spoken to the art teachers about it, she replied,

 Very little because what I left it was very much for the kids to negotiate with their art teachers and, you know, I mentioned to all the art teachers that this was going on, and that they might be approached by some of the kids.

Meagan Scanlan, English teacher, Shipbuilders School

This substitution of decision for action was particularly common at this school, and may be related to the fact that the head had clearly articulated priorities for the school, which did not include cross-subject coursework at that stage. Consequently, time was set aside for the achievement of these other priorities and the planning of interdisciplinary work had to be fitted in around this. In the other schools, there was a much more overt commitment on the part of senior management to cross-curricular innovation. In Lacemakers and Stonemasons it formed a central part of the schools' general 'mission' and was an important feature of TVEI at Stitchers; this commitment was demonstrated not only by the overt support of the heads (for example, the previous head at Stitchers had himself taken part in the interdisciplinary field course) but by the provision of time for teachers to discuss or work on cross-curricular projects.

This pathology was not, however, unique to Shipbuilders. It also occurred, in a different form, at Stitchers, where it may have had an element of 'staking a claim' to it. When the new technology faculty was set up, the head of art had insisted on his department being involved from the beginning. However, according to Kenton Clark, the head of technology, having done this, he did not want to discuss the nature of this involvement, leaving the decisions in this regard to Kenton.

It is unclear why this substitution of decision for action occurs, although it is tempting to speculate that it is due at least in part to the pressure on career-minded teachers to be seen to innovate, combined with a lack of resources to put innovations into practice. It is also possible that it occurs when someone is not yet fully committed to an idea and so 'floats' it to see if anyone else takes it up; this maximises the possibility of credit and minimises the risks of being associated with failure[12] In this case, a decision only appears to have been taken to initiate the decision-making process. At any rate, it is not a particularly recent phenomenon.

 Some observers of the current scene, noting remarkable changes in the rhetoric of pedagogy but little change in practice, believe that many have chosen the wrappings, but few the merchandise, of curriculum innovation.

(MacDonald and Walker, 1976, page 46)

Concluding Remarks

It is unclear why the complexity of decision-making in schools has been so superficially treated in the literature. It may be that it is only in the pressurised world of rapid, multiple, National Curriculum innovation that the issue becomes as problematic as I found it to be. In an atmosphere of hurried and often mistrusted change, teachers may be so overloaded that they are reluctant to take any further risks, wanting to locate the sources of such pressure wholly with outside forces.

The distinction between decision making and decision taking is important here. Decision taking implies both authority and responsibility. However, in the national climate in which this study was undertaken, curriculum authority has been taken away from teachers to an extent never before experienced, while at the same time responsibility has been given the 'edge' implied by appraisal, national testing, publication of examination results and increased competition between schools. Mistakes

---

[12] I am grateful to David Armstrong for this suggestion

have therefore become rather more public than they were, while successes may, in a rapidly moving world, be swept away by the latest change in the regulations[13].

In such a situation, individuals may be reluctant to take risks. Furthermore, because of the interdepartmental nature of cross-subject work, those who would normally have the authority to take curriculum decisions within their specialist area may be less certain that they can do so in this case. Not wanting to be seen as 'empire building', they may find it easier to locate decisions with those who have publicly recognised authority over the generality of the curriculum, the senior management team. This group, however, aware that cross-curricular innovation is likely to lead to personal and pedagogic upheaval, and knowing that participation in decision-making is a prerequisite of feelings of ownership, are at the same time attempting to delegate such authority. Consequently, an impression is given of flight from authority and a move to explanations based on relations of power.

Decision-making in situations of curriculum innovation is an opaque and complex process. It also seems to be under-researched, being almost taken for granted by most studies. Although related to issues of motivation, the decision-making process cannot, as most researchers seem to believe, simply be subsumed in them; the reasons people have for taking particular decisions can only tell you so much about what decisions they actually took, and what choices were, indeed, available to them. This limited study has only scratched the surface of what is a fascinating and complex issue.

---

[13] One near-casualty of this was the original environment course at Lacemakers. The orginal syllabus used was disallowed by SEAC in 1990 and another had to be found for the second run-through of the course.

5 Strategies: Starting, Staying In and Selling

 Some of the things we've done are, sort of, naturally successful, almost, well that's my theory. I mean the art and combined arts business, and some of the other bits and pieces seem to be okay, they've taken root and they're developing really.

CP: What do you mean by 'naturally successful'?

I think there was a natural commitment of the people who are responsible for it, to do it, that way. We aren't asking them to do anything that they don't, that isn't somewhere pretty high on their list of priorities. I think that's important.

Peter Panther, Deputy Head, Lacemakers School, 2/7/91

A key question for those initiating and encouraging any innovation is, how do you get people to start, and once started, how do you ensure continuation? Although in all the schools the proposal to develop cross-disciplinary coursework was accepted by some key people, notably the head and the school co-ordinator, strategies had to be developed to engage the interest of other members of staff, and of students, not just to get the work started with an initial core group but also to enable it to be developed and disseminated more widely. This chapter examines the means by which they sought to do this and the 'selling strategies' used to convince the dubious and pre-empt resistance. From these are drawn recommendations for the carrying out of work of this sort in the future.

Starting

Marris argues that even where change is welcomed, it always involves loss, anxiety and struggle.

 Whether the change is sought or resisted, and happens by chance or design; whether we look at it from the standpoint of reformers or those they manipulate, of individuals or institutions, the response is characteristically ambivalent.

((Marris, 1975), quoted in Fullan, 1991.)

Consequently, for an individual or group to want to take part in an innovation, they need to be able to perceive some benefit. What precisely is needed to attract an individual will depend on that person's agendas (see chapter 3), as will what they actually do to satisfy that need. Fullan (1991) quotes Sarason (1982) as arguing that the new mathematics reforms in the 1960s did not succeed because the teachers were not 'hurting' enough from the previously existing curriculum; consequently there was no individual impetus to change. However, as we have seen, concern about pedagogy is only one of a wide range of reasons given for involvement in curriculum innovation. What matters for those attempting to get such work going in a particular school is that they should find some way of connecting the agendas of those they want to include, to the projected outcomes, so that people feel that there is some point in getting involved in the first place.

 We're looking for fertile ground; in other words we want people who are committed to start with, not people who are brought in because "hey guys, this is a good idea".

Martin Morton, Assistant Curriculum Deputy, Lacemakers School, 30/1/91

All the schools in the Project explicitly began with people who were, at least to some degree, volunteers (although not all recognised themselves as such - see chapter 4). In particular, those at Stitchers and Stonemasons had shown their willingness to participate in cross-disciplinary activities in response to very open invitations:

 I think I went public in some meeting or something like that and said, this was a possibility, would any departments who were interested contact me.

Graham Peacock, TVEI co-ordinator, Stitchers School, 4/12/90

Some were then further encouraged by being given TVEI time to carry out planning and associated activities; at Stitchers this initially consisted of a day, at a local teachers' centre, for those involved. At Shipbuilders, the children's books project was entirely teacher-led, arising out of staffroom discussion. The work there based in special needs was, similarly, instigated by the head of that department out of her concern for particular students. On the other hand, the attempt to combine media studies and information technology was mainly manufactured for the purposes of the Project rather than curriculum or teacher need; this may be a factor in its failure to get going in practice.

At Lacemakers, the situation varied. The combined arts course arose from the teachers involved, and was Peter Panther's paradigm of a 'naturally successful' project. The mathematics/technology module had originated in the minds of senior management, who had then persuaded the departments involved to take part by explicitly addressing the agendas of the department heads. For mathematics, the module removed the necessity to spend mathematics department time and resources on a long piece of coursework; this was a particular concern of theirs, especially regarding the higher ability students. The CDT department were eager to establish a place for technology in the upper school in advance of National Curriculum requirements; it gave the subject a higher profile. The module was then staffed with the acting head of CDT and a mathematics teacher with a particular interest in coursework who was also an examination moderator. This ensured that, at least in the first instance, those committed to the project were involved in planning the work. They were then given a free hand in developing it as they thought best (though Peter Panther continued to complain about its 'unadventurous' nature until well into the second term of operation).

The situation with the integrated humanities and environment courses was less clear. The decision to introduce the supplementary modules and build them into extra GCSEs came from senior management. They then asked for subject-based volunteers to write the modules according to criteria drawn up by Peter Panther and Martin Morton. The two teachers working on the environment course were willing recruits in the sense of having the course 'somewhere pretty high on their list of priorities.' They had been thinking about introducing such a course for some years and thus were ready to respond to Peter Panther's suggestions.

Others, however, did not always see themselves as volunteering freely.

 But no, we weren't, I didn't feel that we were consulted to the extent of "do you think it's a good idea?" or "what do you think about this?" I was consulted: "can you do this?" and the answer was, yes we could do it.

Paul Barker, Head of history, Lacemakers School, 30/1/91

Given the general reluctance of the history department, it is surprising that this course got off the ground at all; it seems to have survived for two reasons. First, the department was characterised by Paul Barker as being made up of people who;

 if you're told to do something you tend to do it. We're not great ones for questioning whether it should be done or not.

Paul Barker, Head of history, Lacemakers School, 30/1/91

Second, while initially requiring considerable time and effort, the teaching and assessment of the integrated humanities modules did not entail any real change in practice. The courses were taught as if they were history, geography, RE or PSE, and the humanities assessment was only unfamiliar for those PSE teachers who were originally from other subject areas.

Staying In

Ruddock (1991) connects teacher commitment to change with a sense of 'ownership' of the innovation. She sees 'ownership' as a unifying slogan which helps those involved feel in control over what was happening.

 The idea of 'ownership' quickly became a key term in the new language of change. It inspired 'collective confidence' (Fullan, 1982) page 295; it made people feel that they were participating in worthwhile communal action.

(Ruddock, 1991, page 123)

Ownership is a key issue not only in starting change but in sustaining it. Because of the use of volunteers, most of the teachers initially involved felt some sense of ownership (although interestingly, Sarah Cordingley, the head of mathematics at Stitchers, seemed to feel ownership without recognising that she had been a volunteer). The crunch came when others had to be included. That everyone has to go through the same process of understanding and assimilation and thus must be allowed the same time for this tends to be ignored by those promoting innovation, who give time for initial development and not for subsequent users. This is partly because of a tendency to regard curriculum innovation as being simply about devising new curricula, not changes in perceptions of one's rôle or in one's pedagogy.

> The difficulty is that educational change is not a single entity even if we keep the analysis at the simplest level of an innovation in a classroom. Innovation is *multidimensional*. There are at least three components or dimensions at stake in implementing any new program or policy: (1) the possible use of new or revised *materials* (direct instructional resources such as curriculum materials or technologies), (2) the possible use of new *teaching approaches* (i.e., new teaching strategies or activities), and (3) the possible alteration of *beliefs* (e.g., pedagogical assumptions and theories underlying particular new policies or programs).

(Fullan, 1991, page 37)

The tendency to ignore the last two of these means that after the initial innovatory group has devised the new materials, subsequent users are not given the time to make the personal changes also required. This means that their ability to share the innovators' understanding of the changes being demanded and consequently to feel ownership of the project with which they are involved, is severely impaired. This leads to a reinterpretation of the new practice in terms of the old, and a tendency to revert back to former, understood ways.

This happened in several cases where the initial work was done by one person or group and passed on to others. At Stitchers, those students who did not go on the field trip had originally carried out a similar study with the mathematics department back at school. However, all the planning for this was done by the head of department and the other mathematics teachers found it difficult to see why she felt it was so important. A previous project involving mathematics and textiles had run into similar problems, with the inter-subject links not being well brought out to students. Although the whole department was ostensibly involved in cross-disciplinary projects, Graham Peacock, the TVEI co-ordinator, still felt that

> I would perhaps like to see it more her department involved in it... I don't know...I don't really know what her department think about cross-curricular issues.
>
> CP: The maths department?
>
> I don't know how much of it is just her or whether she has got the real support of all the staff, you know; that's a difficult one for me to assess.

Graham Peacock, Stitchers School, 4/12/90

At Lacemakers, where most of the projects were in their second year or more, as staff became involved who had not taken part in initial planning, there was a tendency to what Peter Panther, the deputy head, called 'reverting'. A change in personnel, replacing the teachers originally involved in the planning with others who were handed a 'finished' innovation, meant that the work was no longer carried out as originally intended. Handy refers to this phenomenon as

> what Americans call the NIH syndrome (Not Invented Here). The data and the ideas are alien to those who would have to carry them out, and are therefore rejected.

(Handy, 1985, page 345)

This happened in the Lacemakers mathematics/technology course:

 I think that they have actually reverted somewhat. I hadn't realised that was the case, but we took one member of staff off[14] and put somebody else on and they promptly switched it around and took the practical work out.

[...]

CP: So what are they doing?

Well they've kept it out of the workshops. See, they get about twelve, thirteen weeks, three periods a week...[...]...Barry started delivering and then he had to come off it to do something else because of Tom Warren's secondment, and that really spoilt it I think, and I think it is important that practical work is in there and I shall intend to go back and make sure that it goes in.

Peter Panther, Lacemakers School, 2/7/91

In an attempt to prevent this 'reversion' going any further, the two teachers who had set up the project were planning an in-service session for those likely to be involved in the future, using TVEI funding.

In general, however, the projects were surprisingly robust to staff changes, within the short time that the schools were studied. This was achieved by a number of conscious and unconscious strategies on the part of those responsible for the development.

At Lacemakers, the combined arts course had been running for some time mainly with the two initial staff members, but a second art teacher (the school had only one drama teacher) was being brought into the team-teaching for one lesson a week, as well as taking responsibility for the module that supplemented the course. He was supported in the personal changes this entailed by his head of department, Martin Morton, who was very conscious of how he himself had been changed through working with drama, and how difficult it could be for the individual. As a result, he felt that

 I'm quite sure if I dropped out and Malcolm who is in the fourth year slotted into my place, that would function perfectly well, I can't see any problem with that at all. And he has come back and said I don't know how I'm going to cope with it, but I want to get involved in this drama. But not everybody would do that. Not everybody would feel confident enough I think, or secure enough in themselves.

Martin Morton, Lacemakers School, 12/11/90

Although this course was the most integrated and required the most personal change for the teachers concerned, it seemed to be robust, and had been running for several years, albeit with few personnel changes.

At Stonemasons, there was a conscious strategy to spread change slowly by person to person diffusion. Innovative departments, such as English, were paired with those, such as history, that wanted to change their practice. This was done on a one-to-one basis, each teacher being given a particular person to work with and time to meet. A key factor in this was the personal commitment of the

---

[14] Barry Johnson, the CDT teacher jointly responsible for devising the project, had to take over an 'A' level class mid-year. He was replaced by a junior member of his department.

head, who was a member of the history department and took part in this exercise. At the same time, the library was improved to encourage staff to try resource-based learning:

> I surveyed all the staff when we first started looking at the library and trying to turn it into a resource centre, and surveyed the staff with the idea that if I went to the staff and said, we're going to try and convert it into a resource centre, what would you want to see in it? What would you like to see in there? and if we could get that then it would encourage the staff to think, well we've asked for this and it's there now, we're going to use it. So that was I trying to get them to contribute more to the resource centre. I think it's a slow sort of spread of ideas, you can't convert everybody straight away, just different ideas.

John Blackwell, geography teacher, Stonemasons School, 25/1/91

Towards the end of the study, plans were being made to decentralise resources so that they would be more easily accessible to departments, though John Blackwell feared this might make cross-disciplinary links less likely.

At Shipbuilders, the children's book task continued to take place, though with less co-ordination between the departments as time went on. After a while, only two teachers, Sally Brightday, the head of art, and Jenny Sims, an English teacher, were discussing the work as it was presented to students and carried out by them. As a result, apart from that done with these two teachers, there was a decreasing amount of work produced that could be credited for both subjects; the drawings done in English lessons, in particular, lacked the evidence of preparation and preliminary sketching required by the art department. Links between English and other subjects co-ordinated by the special needs department continued, but were very much the work of the head of department, Hilary Blondel. She was finding it increasingly hard to work with the English department as it was often difficult for them to find time for meetings, and was beginning to look elsewhere. However, she felt that cross-subject work needed to have a higher profile in the school as a whole if real progress were to be made.

> What I need to do is, in a sense I think it needs all heads of faculty to come together and actually we need to know...I think there are school based implications, and that we all need to know, the eight of us need to know what other people are actually doing within their subject areas, because although this particular project has actually made people realise that there are overlaps with other subject areas, I still think there are probably a great many more, and I don't think we should rely on the pupils to identify the overlap, we should have a clearer picture of what the syllabus of each course is, and actually see it for ourselves. So I would, I suppose my opinion would be initially to ask Peter Jones, who's the deputy head for curriculum, to actually...give it more status if you like, by putting it on agendas of senior committee meetings and actually encouraging that sort of discourse amongst us at the moment.

Hilary Blondel, Shipbuilders School, 4/2/91

This did not happen during the period in which I worked with the school, apart from a meeting in September 1990 at which I was introduced to the faculty and pastoral heads. The head had other priorities and was reluctant to give meeting time to projects that had not already proved themselves.

As the only school of the four where no time was given to staff for liaison meetings, it is perhaps not surprising that relatively little liaison took place here.

The mathematics/science/geography project at Stitchers continued as a self-contained field course, and was expected to do so even after all but one of those who had actually worked on it had left. This was of course partly because it was based on a well-established part of the geography curriculum, and so the trip itself would have happened anyway. However, TVEI time was also given, particularly in the second year of the project, to release people from teaching so that they could meet. In the same way as projects continued at least nominally at Lacemakers because they were built into the timetable, it is to be anticipated that this course would continue, but as the geography department has been almost completely replaced and a new science teacher is to be involved, what actually happens may be quite different.

The school co-ordinators in Fordingshire and Camberside were also supported from outside by groups set up by advisory staff. In Fordingshire, the co-ordinators of all the local Project schools met with each other, Jeannie Silcock (the LEA co-ordinator) and me, in one of the schools, for about one morning a term. These meetings were used to provide a forum for the raising of problems and issues and made the rôle of the school co-ordinator less isolated. We were also fortunate in that the integrated humanities moderator for Lacemakers was the co-ordinator at another local Project school, and so the school was supported in the development of this course by ongoing contact with and understanding from him. In Camberside the meetings occurred after school, again about once a term, and were held in a teachers' centre. This group had in fact pre-dated the introduction of the Project into the county and had been the means by which the schools were recruited. Despite the need to travel quite long distances to get to these meetings, they were well attended not only by staff from the Project schools but also other interested teachers.

In setting up the Project we had intended that advisory staff would support all schools in this way. However, with changes in advisory rôles and the advent of local financial management, very few of our original LEA co-ordinators were still in post at the end of the Project. it is notable that the two most successful counties in terms of teacher commitment and ongoing and developing projects, as well as dissemination between schools, were Fordingshire and Camberside, where schools were supported by the same individuals throughout.

Selling

 ...there is a strong tendency to "oversell" innovations in order to obtain funding or to get them adopted by policy-makers, teachers and others. The gap between the benefits promised and those received is usually very large, even in situations where good intentions exist.

(Fullan, 1991, page 129)

Selling is about matching the innovation to the agendas of those who one hopes will carry it out or those who have the potential to block it. Both are important, and both have to be handled with care. In particular, it is essential that those supporting an innovation are not so eager to get it introduced that they promise benefits that cannot really be supported. Fullan points out that 'strong commitment to a particular change may be a barrier to setting up an effective process of change' (Fullan, 1991, page 95); this is particularly the case if commitment leads to overselling and a reluctance to meet and change with the objections and agendas of others. This may have been a factor in a development reported by Paul Barker, the head of history at Lacemakers:

> I think in many ways staff were, not exactly anti the King's College project, but they were led to believe it was going to actually cut down on the amount of work they had to do and it hasn't done that.

Paul Barker, Lacemakers School, 30/1/91

At the same time, it is also important to be aware that the change process itself may be a significant factor in spreading an innovation; a small group of initial volunteers may be able to bring others in by virtue of their success.

There are two facets to the selling of innovations. The first concerns the persuasion of those who will have to carry them out, in this context, the teachers. Given that lasting change is more likely to take place if participation is voluntary, those promoting innovations have to have some sort of strategy to encourage volunteers, while not 'overselling', resulting in disappointment later. The second facet concerns the 'consumers'. If curriculum changes are far-reaching or very public, they have to be sold to students, parents and governors. Failure to develop strategies for either at an early stage can result in resistance if valued parts of the status quo are threatened.

Most of the school co-ordinators began simply by asking for volunteers and then doing no further selling, though Graham Peacock was able to pre-empt objections that there was no time to meet by providing funding to allow staff to be released from teaching to plan the new projects. However, the deputy head at Lacemakers, Peter Panther, who was trying to instigate larger structural changes, had a variety of explicit strategies, both to encourage people to take part and to pre-empt mass refusal. As described above, he took the trouble to incorporate aspects of departmental agendas into at least some of his plans, explicitly pointing out the potential benefits and striking bargains with heads of department. At the same time, he was aware of the ways in which group dynamics can result in refusal to consider something new, and so presented his ideas very carefully. For example, when looking for volunteers for the Year 7 tutor team (who would have to teach 20% of the Year 7 timetable in an interdisciplinary way),

> instead of making a public announcement, please we want tutors, and give people the chance to sort of put a group nose up at it and say no, we don't want to be tutors, we're actually approaching people individually and asking them if they want to do it.

Peter Panther, Lacemakers School, 17/1/91

The initial planning stages for this were carried out by the directors of studies (DOS) for each year, who had only recently been appointed when the management structure of the school was changed to reflect an increased emphasis on pastoral work. Again, he took care explicitly to warn this group of the potential dangers:

The DOS people we appointed for the cross-curriculum, cross-curricular responsibility; we spent ages talking to them about the problems they might get. They were tempted to gallop on and start making pronouncements about what was going to take place. No, that's not a good idea because if you upset the departments you're going to get no co-operation at all. You're going to be on your own.

Peter Panther, Lacemakers School, 2/10/90

It is also important to sell innovations to students, parents and governors, particularly in the early stages, when the benefits may not be apparent. All of the schools thought about this, though some had more explicit strategies than others. For Tony Higginbotham, the head of Stonemasons, it was not so much the Flexible Learning project that he wanted to sell, as education:

 I think Flexible Learning will help, in that it will very much more motivate the pupil because they'll get involved in their work; that should raise motivation and then learning, you know, raise achievement. That's how I would see it working, in that if they're really gripped by what they're doing then that will push them on to better things, and you know they start to value education.

Tony Higginbotham, Stonemasons School, 25/1/91

Consequently, the selling of the Flexible Learning project was incorporated into his general drive to persuade 'the community to value education more' and publicised in his regular school newsletter which emphasised the achievements of current and past students. This strategy was not dissimilar to that used by the English department at Shipbuilders, who saw the children's books project as more or less selling itself; the students enjoyed doing it and did not therefore have to be persuaded to give time to it. At the same time they saw the visit to the primary school, which started off the project, as being a significant motivating factor.

At Stitchers, the interdisciplinary work was explicitly sold to the students as saving them time, particularly regarding their mathematics coursework. This was also the case with the Lacemakers mathematics/technology course. At this school there was concern that students would not participate fully in modules that did not contribute to examination passes, and so there was an attempt to build this in explicitly wherever possible, even though these components had originally been included in the interests of giving them a broader general education. Where this was not possible, there were explicit attempts to make the work as enjoyable as possible:

 ...we could take music out, but we actually quite like it there, we think it provides, it does provide a balance of experiences for the children, that is what is coming across. The kids don't...they don't like too many modules which don't have an outcome and if they go to a module which doesn't have an outcome they like it to be clear and they like it to be active and provided that that happens then it's OK. You know.

Peter Panther, deputy head, Lacemakers School, 12/11/90

Because of Peter Panther's belief that parental agendas were mainly to do with numbers of GCSE passes, this was emphasised in the promotion of the modular structure, and particularly of the supplementary modules, although once the courses were underway, this was not stressed so explicitly to students. This led to problems, because some parents (and students) became very aware of how many GCSEs could be taken, and there was concern on the part of the school that maximising examination outcomes was affecting option choice. When students studying a lot of subjects later ran into difficulties, individual staff members sometimes re-thought the sales strategy to emphasise higher grades in higher status subjects.

 ...the way we sold it, and the way we sort of shimmied them along was to really say well look, ok maybe you won't get top grade in your environmental studies, but it will push you up a grade in biology, or push you up a grade in geography, I mean you might be able to use the environment work in maybe chemistry, or somewhere else where a question will come along and you will be able to that and maybe somebody else won't.

Roy Saunders, head of geography, Lacemakers School, 4/6/91

A further strategy in the selling of the modular system at Lacemakers was that it explicitly addressed the issue of how to fit the quart of the National Curriculum into the pint pot of the timetable. The senior management at the school were in favour of the idea that every student should follow a broad and balanced curriculum for the full five years and the advent of the National Curriculum provided an impetus to attempt to put this into practice. They saw the 'lead time' before the full curriculum became compulsory in the upper school as an opportunity to try out different models for doing this, starting by insisting that all students should do at least one module of music, technology (either a technology subject as a full GCSE or the mathematics/technology module) and modern languages in year 10 or 11. They also adopted integrated science for all (which was county policy). Although the senior management had wanted to do this anyway, it was sold to parents and students as being part of meeting National Curriculum requirements. As these were relaxed during 1990-91, this became an increasing problem for Peter Panther, who wanted to retain these components but was unsure if they would now be so popular with parents.

 I think we do need time to really think about it, think what we want and how the expectations of the children and the parents will actually play a part; we need to be able to justify whatever we're doing, and be happy ourselves that we're actually pushing things in the right direction. But what we don't want is an imbalance, so we might decide that yes, we want them all to have an art experience, but then what we're saying is that's us, no one else is saying we should do it. What backing have we got for it, it has to be very enjoyable, where it has to slot in naturally to other experiences that we think are important.

CP: Because otherwise you are actually standing up and saying that the Secretary of State says we don't have to but we're going to make you.

Yeah, which I think would be a mistake.

Peter Panther, Lacemakers School, 17/1/91

What began as a convenient sales strategy was in danger of developing into a hostage to fortune.

Conclusions

In planning educational innovations it is essential to recognise the multidimensional nature of change. This does not mean necessarily that all planned changes have to address all dimensions, but that they will not be particularly radical or far-reaching if they do not. The integrated humanities course at Lacemakers, for example, had the limited aim of giving all students experience in two humanities subjects, with the carrot of an examination outcome; changes in practice or in personal beliefs were not necessary for this to happen. However, more radical changes need fertile ground and voluntary participation if they are not to meet with either compliance in name only or general resistance. All expected to be involved, whether in the short or long term, need to be brought to see the need for change and take part in fashioning it, and this takes time.

Time for teachers to meet, discuss and plan is also crucial, and not only in the early stages. All concerned have to go through the processes involved in changing, otherwise later adopters will superficially implement the more visible aspects of the innovation, such as the curriculum materials, and not think through, understand or own the ideas that underlie them. This is particularly important when change is imposed from outside, as it is unlikely to coincide with individuals' readiness for innovation; in this case there is likely to be a period of mourning for former practice followed by a transition phase in which people prepare themselves for the new beginning (Redway, 1992). If this is not appreciated, resistance to the new practice is unlikely to be overcome. This has been apparent in the case of the introduction of design and technology, where the upheaval of innovation has reawakened, in some CDT teachers, feelings of loss of their original craft teaching not dealt with in the move to CDT (Paechter, 1995).

Those people initiating and co-ordinating change also need support, and in particular the opportunity to meet with others in the same situation on a regular basis. This should not be seen as a substitute for giving all concerned in the work the opportunity to talk through issues and problems. However, the findings of the Project suggest that inter-school meetings between co-ordinators, supported by LEA advisory staff, can be effective in supporting the development of cross-disciplinary links.

In 'selling' innovations it is essential to find ways of connecting the anticipated outcomes with the agendas of those to whom one is attempting to persuade that the change is a good idea. However, it is important to take care not to 'oversell' and suggest that agendas will be fulfilled, if this is unlikely to be the case. Meaningful change is hard, time-consuming and disruptive; it is better that a few well-thought-through and useful innovations take root than that a larger number are superficially accepted or even seen as imposed, cause distress and disturbance and finally do not result in changes in practice.

6 Managing Cross-Curricular Work: structural and personal dimensions

A key concern for those responsible for managing the introduction of curriculum change within a school is that it should be both successfully developed in the short term, and survive the initial innovative period. This means that the innovation has to be incorporated both into the normal life of the school as a whole and into the everyday practices of the individual teachers involved. In the case study schools, this concern and how to overcome it has two key dimensions: implementation through curriculum structures such as the timetable and working with a group of key people. This paper explores issues around these two dimensions and the difficulties experienced by managers in taking account of and operating equally with both. This will be done mainly through looking at the approaches of senior managers in the two schools at which management strategies for the introduction of cross-curricular coursework form a pair of contrasting extremes: Lacemakers and Stonemasons.

The analysis comes largely from interviews with management figures in both schools. At Lacemakers, the key people were Peter Panther, the curriculum deputy head, and Martin Morton, the assistant deputy responsible for curriculum. The central trio at Stonemasons were the head, Tony Higginbotham, Jim Branestawm, one of the three deputy heads, and Gordon Swallow, the TVEI co-ordinator. In both schools these were the people who took the initiative in managing the introduction of cross-curricular coursework, and it is their perceptions of what might be the most effective strategies for thorough, robust innovation that I want to explore.

The origins and importance of the structures/persons interface are fairly straightforward. If an innovation is to take place at all, key figures are needed, who are both willing and able to effect change. Such change agents may not only be able to alter their own work but can also be instrumental in supporting change in others' practices. Educational institutions tend to be fairly settled, and enthusiasm is needed if teachers are to be prepared to undergo the upheaval necessary to change previously established methods and routines. Marsh et al (1990) locate the impetus for participation in school-based curriculum development (which they describe as a teacher-initiated, grass-roots phenomenon) in teachers' current levels of job satisfaction, describing each individual as having their own configuration of driving and restraining forces. At the same time, however, curriculum structures will be need to be adapted to support the continuation of the innovation through personnel changes. Marsh et al also point out that while teachers who are highly motivated to introduce curriculum change can enthuse other staff, they are also a destabilising influence, particularly because of their own subsequent career shifts (Fullan, 1991) (due to being successful innovators). Peter Panther echoes this belief:

You tend to lose the key people. You *always* lose the key people because they are the people who are going to get the jobs elsewhere, because other people see those skills, and abilities, and enthusiasms, and ..."oh, yeah!" We lost Jane Partridge, she's only been in the job a year and working with Tim Ball in the Year 7 work... brilliant, and that's it. She's just started to be, you know, really shape up getting into the job, and now she's gone.

Peter Panther, Lacemakers School, 2/7/91

There is thus a strong pressure on management to attempt to incorporate curriculum change into formal structures, in an attempt to ensure longevity.

It is clear that both the structures and the persons approaches are concerned with structuring, but that with one it is formal curriculum structures that are the focus, while with the other it is the facilitation of encounters between persons. The approach taken by a school needs to reflect some sort of balance between the two; an overemphasis on one can lead to problems with the other. However, because they are aligned with different preferred management styles, there is a tendency for those responsible for promoting innovations to concern themselves with one while playing down or ignoring the importance of the other. The two complementary dimensions then begin to be seen as dichotomous and the imbalance in emphasis may become exaggerated in management rhetoric. An individual manager's preference for structural or personal approaches is also in some ways emblematic of their style in general (Ball, 1987); it can both highlight the advantages and illuminate the drawbacks of particular management approaches.

Timetable Structures: Lacemakers School

The approach taken to cross-subject work at Lacemakers was from the start firmly located in the realm of formal curriculum structures. This reflects Peter Panther's belief that

 you have to provide other structures and ways for them to work to get departments to change.

Peter Panther, Lacemakers School, 17/12/90 (field notes)

As described in Chapter One, in order to give more flexibility in Years 10 and 11, the school had introduced a modular curriculum in these years, and had further developed this idea by creating a bank of 'supplementary modules', some of which were optional and some compulsory. For example, all students had to take at least one module of modern languages and one of music during the two year period. Other modules were taken to 'balance' the overall diet of an individual student and/or to provide extra GCSE courses. In particular, everyone (in theory at least) took integrated humanities by combining their main humanities subject with a supplementary module of history or geography (whichever was not being taken as a full subject), PSE work and RE; some students had also used this as a way to avoid doing either history or geography GCSE at all, by taking supplementary modules in both subjects. It was also possible to take GCSE environment through a similar combination of science and geography. There was, in addition, a specially designed cross-curricular technology module taken by most students, which, as well as ensuring that all students did some sort of technology in the upper school (three years earlier than required by the National Curriculum) also provided a major piece of mathematics coursework. A more longstanding course, taken by about forty students, was combined arts, which was timetabled to be team-taught by an art and a drama teacher and which allowed students to enter for both art (theatre design) and drama GCSE; students used the same pieces of coursework for both subjects.

In starting off this work, Peter Panther, the deputy head responsible for the curriculum, began with the timetable, building in the space for the supplementary modules and then, as hew saw it, leaving it to departments or individuals to offer suggestions:

> We didn't push people to run the modules. We said, this pool is available and what we want to do is to deliver National Curriculum entitlement, but there is scope and flexibility for some interested people to do different things. And what we found is people sort of came and almost demanded to participate.

Peter Panther, Lacemakers School, 2/10/90

Those people who elected to provide a supplementary module had to design it to conform to often quite closely specified criteria laid down by himself and Martin Morton, but there was, in theory at least, no compulsion to take part. One of the advantages of this, as he saw it, is that were are no hostages to fortune on either side:

> The attraction of the modules is you ask someone to prepare something and be quite specific about what you want and they can say yes I'm prepared to do it or no, I don't think so, you know, I'll leave it this time. It doesn't make any difference because you can replace it with something else.

Peter Panther, Lacemakers School, 2/10/90

On the other hand, this perception was not shared by all the staff involved, and being asked to devise something according to Peter and Martin's preordained structure (which included, for example, a requirement to fit in with an overall theme) was not always welcomed. Paul Barker, the head of history, saw the starting point for negotiation as being placed by senior management at a rather different place from where he would prefer to see it. By the time the staff were involved in discussion the structures were already in place; negotiations centred around the content of the modules, not whether there should be supplementary modules in the first place.

> I mean I'm sure they would argue and say that it was discussed, but it depends on what your point for starting the discussion is, and I certainly had the opinion right from the beginning that this was in. It's the same with the cross curricular initiatives in Year 7[15].
>
> I mean we spent three or four meetings talking about that and going round and round in circles and in the end at one of the meetings I said, look is this in or isn't it? You know is this structure in place? And I was told, yes the structure is, and I said, what are we talking about, I said, lets sit down and get it done, because you could spend the rest of your life arguing about whether you should do something.

Paul Barker, Lacemakers School, 30/1/91

---

[15] in which 20% of Year 7 students' timetable was to be used for cross-curricular work.

A similar point was made by Colin Fishbourne, the mathematics teacher involved in the technology module:

We were really basically pushed into doing it 'cos they wanted to do entitlement technology, and no-one could think of what to do in entitlement technology, and Peter said to Bill, "Would you like to run an OET[16] in technology?" and Bill said, "Oh I could consider doing that" and the next thing we knew it's on the timetable.

Colin Fishbourne, Lacemakers School, 2/10/90

As a result, staff enthusiasm for an innovation may not run as deep as senior management might hope:

I think everyone was quite enthusiastic for it in theory, but practice was something else [...] I think they did have an enthusiasm for it, but it was in the meeting rather than outside, it just...went. I mean to a certain extent that's what you get, you can actually serve people up to be interested in something but ... .

Peter Panther, Lacemakers School, 2/7/91

Related to this is the need to find suitable people to develop the innovation in the first place; if too much has been built into the structure than can be handled by the more enthusiastic members of staff this can be a problem (Fullan, 1991) During the year 1990-91 both Peter Panther and Martin Morton were preoccupied with developing a cross-curricular course for Year 7 students that would take up 20% of their timetable and be taught by the tutor team. In order to ensure that the first year of this went as well as possible, suitable tutors (in terms of subject background - they wanted a broad range - as well as commitment to the project) had to be found, if necessary from other year groups.

It's very difficult to get a proper balance without poaching people from all over the place. I mean we've said to Year 7, next year's Year 7 Director of Studies, you know you've got to poach, you've got to poach. So in theory the year eleven team that's going in should be the basis of the Year 7 team because they're all free. But we don't actually want them all. So he's got to really poach from other years.

Peter Panther, Lacemakers School, 17/1/91

We're looking for fertile ground, in other words we want people who are committed to start with, not people who are brought in because "hey guys, this is a good idea".

Martin Morton, Lacemakers School, 30/1/91

---

[16] Open-Ended Task, part of SMP mathematics coursework

Some otherwise key people (such as the only drama teacher) were unavailable because of their commitments in other parts of the school. Meanwhile, others were looking for a way out:

> What's happened now is that staff are on the run from for example National Curriculum technology and there are a couple who have said... when they were asked which tutor team they want to be in, they have said, "Any year but Year 7. We want to keep well away from Year 7, all this nasty National Curriculum." They are the staff who would naturally form a tutor team for next year. Now they discover that its worse than National Curriculum technology because we are asking them to do National Curriculum technology and 20% cross-curricular work.

Peter Panther, Lacemakers School, 12/11/90

Over time, this 20% cross-curricular provision will catch up with the modular timetable in the upper school, leaving staff who would rather not be involved with nowhere to run from the inexorability of the curriculum structure. This lack of personal commitment from those who were not initially involved in an innovation can mean that, while it remains in place in structural terms, it may not continue to run as planned. Peter Panther was already beginning to see this happen with some of the modular courses as they ran into their second year:

> The first year where we set it up we were very careful who we staffed the modules with, so for example Sarah Perry was doing the languages bit with Mark Patterson, and they worked together very well, and I think that experience was successful. This year we've got a much weaker team on it, and it tends to have reverted to people charging around with video camcorders and things, not really achieving anything much at all.

Peter Panther, Lacemakers School, 2/7/91

So although the innovation was built into the curriculum structure deliberately in order to ensure its longevity, it may not long remain in the form originally intended.

It would be misleading to suggest that at Lacemakers innovation occurred only through curriculum structures; it is more that there it was believed both that structures themselves provided space for innovation to take place and that only if a supporting structure is in place will any individual project survive. The combined arts course, for example, began when two teachers started working together in the lower school and asked for timetable provision to be made so that they could continue this in Years 10 and 11. There was an emphasis on persons at a more meta-level, coming before the curricular structuring that was the overt focus of the school's approach. Martin Morton and Peter Panther worked particularly closely, and it was their *personal* interaction that led to the development of the *structural* innovations.

A lot of it, as it does, comes out of informal discussion, you know when you get together after school and you just talk about how courses can be structured.

CP: Is that just you and Peter, then, or other people?

Yes, generally. [...] You know, that's been one of our gripes actually, that there isn't space within the school day or a willingness outside of it for people at the top end to actually sit down and talk about the kind of issues that do affect, in my view, affect the curriculum, which are talking about the way in which you want to develop projects, and the impact this is going to have on the education within the school, the exciting stuff really. [...]...it tends to be seen as your responsibility, you go and do it, you know those two people go in that room and talk strange things for a long time and emerge with ideas, and we get people and corner them and sort of say, how about doing this, and they say, all right, or no, or do I have to, or whatever.

Martin Morton, Lacemakers School, 30/1/91

Peter Panther was also aware that working with structures alone was not enough. Here he both articulates the difficulties with and clarifies the relationship between the structures and persons dimensions.

 It does rely on communication of course, though. All we're saying in making the space or trying to make things happen by actually providing... I think it's a concern that unless you provide a firm context of something to happen, it's likely to disappear, and I've haven't found any evidence contrary to that. I haven't, honestly. It might sound cynical but there aren't. It's down to people. I mean if you rely on people then you've got to have a recruitment policy whereby you take somebody on and they are committed to doing the things that you want to do. That isn't easy, and you can't always judge those things in the interview, but if you're changing a school, if you're coming into a school with a brief to change it, then you're inheriting a whole range of issues aren't you?

:

:

:

But all the drawbacks I've explained to you are where personnel's changed, aren't they, yes all right, well thank you. Yes that's made its point...it's not just about making space for things, you do talk to people at the same time. I would claim that actually having the space there that needs an input is an advantage because you are really getting a commitment to it.

Peter Panther, Lacemakers School, 2/7/91

Interpersonal Interactions: Stonemasons School

In contrast to Lacemakers, Stonemasons School approached cross-disciplinary work from an entirely person-focused perspective, starting with the individual student and working through the Flexible Learning Project. Flexible Learning has at its centre the idea that students should be enabled to direct their own work as far as possible, and so cross-subject work in this school took the form of individually negotiated joint projects. In examining the way that the school's senior management approached cross-subject coursework, I will therefore focus on how they started work on the introduction of Flexible Learning.

In the initial stages, there was nothing built into curriculum structures as such; the structuring that occurred was of meetings between people and time for individuals and groups to devise teaching strategies and learning materials. Personal commitment was seen as the key factor from the start.

 And I actually just started off by having a group of six teachers, doing approaches to teaching and learning, just looking at what made effective learning and so on; we had a little project and then that finally turned into a support group.

Jim Branestawm, Stonemasons School, 13/12/90

This structuring of person-encounters rather than the curriculum itself was part of the more general management style of the head, Tony Higginbotham. When asked about setting up formal structures to facilitate change, he focused on interpersonal support and the way that this can operate through line management.

 CP: In terms of actual Flexible Learning, in terms of how the school can facilitate that sort of work, are you doing anything structural, or very much working with individuals?

No, we are doing things structural and you know, we put into systems, when it's a good management systems in the school, which should support the development, and well, are supporting it. [...] We also have a line management system: I manage the English and modern languages departments, that would involve some support, some supervision, depending on.... So I think that there is much more of a structure there to support the development of Flexible Learning in particular which is one of our priorities.

Tony Higginbotham, Stonemasons School, 25/1/91

This emphasis on supporting development through interpersonal contact was also illustrated by his introduction, shortly after he arrived at the school in June 1990, of after-school workshops for departments to work on curriculum matters. These were a new feature in the school and were valued by staff for their role in allowing innovation to be percolated slowly but steadily through and between departments. Pauline Hardy, the head of English and one of the central group of teachers working on Flexible Learning, explained the advantages of this process:

 It is much easier to develop new ideas now, because I can also, the other good thing is that our new head has arranged that we have workshops very regularly every week after school, with the department. Which is brilliant. So it means that you can develop new ideas and you can actually sit and talk things out. They take a long while to get through, but gradually, you know, because you are discussing this all the time, things are being implemented, people say: yes I have been thinking of open study, yes, I will try it with literature, and gradually it's a slow process of persuading people, because it isn't actually, it isn't essential in our syllabus.

Pauline Hardy, Stonemasons School, 22/11/90

This may be contrasted with a remark made by the TVEI co-ordinator at Stitchers School. This school had more of a balance between structures and persons, but with different emphases at different levels. The interpersonal communication tended to be between heads of department (for which structural support was given in the form of TVEI-funded time). Those heads of department were then expected to structure the curriculum within the department in such a way as to facilitate change. Consequently, while the head of mathematics was a key figure in the development of cross-disciplinary coursework, the rest of the department found it harder to get involved:

> There were certainly problems in terms of the way it was administered, and communicated through to the departments I think it got ... it got itself a bad name in the maths department. Um .. you know .. I think .. I don't know if whether any of that's been repaired or not and it needs to be sort of imbibed into their sort of curriculum and their schemes of work and everything and I don't know to what degree it has been.
>
> *Graham Peacock, Stitchers School, 4/12/90*

At Stonemasons, innovative approaches could be passed from department to department in an almost ad hoc manner. John Blackwell, a geography teacher centrally involved in the development of the Flexible Learning Project, and Gordon Swallow, the TVEI co-ordinator, both refer to personal influences on the development of the work in the history department:

> I mean, there were two teachers doing geography, and a chap [a history teacher]...[...]...I was doing one half of the lesson, I had two periods a week. Because I had TVEI time I lost one of those and he took over the other half, so it's the same group but he had them for one period and I had them for another period, and that, the ideas of self supported study I passed onto him, because it was useful for him to do that, [...] so he picked that up and moved the ideas across to history. So it's my ideas in history that are being used.
>
> *John Blackwell, Stonemasons School, 25/1/91*

> History has really come on quite dramatically this year, in a way pushed by that project that Jim devised, but also equally I think because Tony Higginbotham's [the headteacher] come into the History.
>
> *Gordon Swallow, Stonemasons School, 25/5/91*

At the same time, departments were also put into supportive pairings by senior management, individual teachers working together in twos to develop and disseminate new practice.

For the senior management at Stonemasons, structuring was thus seen as a facilitating mechanism for the development of departments and the individuals in them, rather than a way of writing the timetable to facilitate particular sorts of innovation. The reasoning behind this seems to be that if people are committed to a particular change, then it will become an embedded part of their practice and the drift away from initial practice seen in some areas at Lacemakers will be less likely to occur. On the other hand, the process of change can seem very slow, the continuation of the innovation may depend on a low level of staff turnover, and the priorities of the managers may well become lost as the alternative agendas of the teachers involved take over. In this situation it can be difficult for managers to have much say in what changes take place in practice, apart from supporting or failing to support ideas with meeting time.

Well, as far as the GCSE thing's concerned, the one thing that's sort of worried me about what we've been doing is the fact that we haven't got the multiple accreditation thing really off the ground, but that was really the way things sorted out. The individuals who actually came to those earlier meetings didn't seem to latch on to that as being a lead for them or a way forward.

Gordon Swallow, TVEI coordinator, Stonemasons School, 13/5/91

Balancing dimensions

It is clear that polarisation towards one or other of the structures and persons dimensions brings with it weaknesses inherent in an exclusive focus. The result in either case is that senior managers are unable to achieve the changes they seek. A focus on structures, while allowing rapid and far-reaching change (it would have been hard to innovate to the degree Lacemakers did without the structural changes they put in place), can result in feelings of pressure and coercion on the part of staff, with a consequent falling-off of commitment to the innovation and the possibility that it may eventually be in place in name only. Working entirely through persons, on the other hand, while encouraging a deeper commitment from participants, takes a long time, may not result in what the managers intended, and leaves the curriculum vulnerable to the career moves of key individuals.

However, because the two dimensions are associated with different management styles, managers seem in practice to perceive them as dichotomous and find it hard to operate with both at once. In doing this, they leave themselves open to the weaknesses inherent in each position. Whether this tendency to polarisation can be escaped is unclear. It may be that the choice of strategy is so embedded in the general management style of the person adopting it that alternative choices are not in practice possible (Ball, 1987). The dichotomy is thus seen not as something about which one can make decisions, but rather as 'the obvious strategy' versus an alternative that at best may seem unrealistic and at worst be incomprehensible. At least in the first instance, we need to find ways to help senior managers to recognise the importance of both sides of the structures/persons balance, rather than treating it as a dichotomy that can only be dealt with by going for one dimension or the other.

7 Assessment-focused Subject Subcultures

 Nobody in this school has got a complete oversight of what's happening environmentally, curriculum-wise. You know they turn to us two, but no, we're MEG environment, or NEA[17] environment. We haven't got time to go and discover what's happening elsewhere, we're too busy throwing fuel on the fire, keeping those kids going.

Robert Partington, biology teacher, Lacemakers School, 4/6/91

In a traditional subject-based curriculum the division of school knowledge into subject areas is bound up with the initiation and socialisation of teachers into subject subcultural groupings. Within these, there is a further division into competing ideological segments (such as those favouring Schools Council history, NATE-style English or investigationally-based mathematics) (Ball and Lacey, 1980; Cooper, 1985; Goodson, 1985b; St.John-Brooks, 1983). Such subcultures represent contested but more-or-less consensus views about such things as the nature of the subject, the way it should be taught, the role of the teacher and what might be expected of the student. These sub-cultural givens allow subject teachers or segmental groupings of subject teachers to participate in a common understanding of the nature of teaching and learning and hence to communicate with each other using a shared language which reflects these underlying assumptions. The subject sub-cultural group thus acts as a unifying focus for teachers, out of which can be developed ideas about pedagogy and assessment and within which an individual can locate her or himself with a reasonable degree of reliability. This unifying focus also acts as a pressure on the individual to conform to subcultural norms, as access to promotion can depend on one's ability to present oneself as a fully initiated and conforming member of the subject group.

Although the subject subculture is both fluid and contested, it is nevertheless increasingly focused around and influenced by the content of examination syllabuses and the processes by which they are assessed. Barnes and Seed point out that

 The relationship between the process of learning in the classroom and public examinations at 16+ is both close and complex.

going on to say that

---

[17] Midland Examining Group and Northern Examination Association.

Examination papers...offer to teacher and taught the most persuasive arguments about what model of the subject is appropriate, what should go on in lessons, what knowledge, skills and activities should be emphasised and what can safely be ignored.

(Barnes and Seed, 1984, page 263)

The effect of this is, as Reid points out, that

 school programmes tend towards topical uniformity within politically united or culturally homogeneous territories ....[especially]...where national systems of assessment or accreditation result in *de facto* limitations on acceptable practice

(Reid, 1984, page 72)

The effects of assessment schemes on teachers' subcultural stances have not, however, sufficiently been taken into account in the literature. This may be because most of the work carried out pre-dates GCSE and the widespread appearance of substantial amounts of teacher-assessed coursework in Mode One (Examining Group written) syllabuses. Although it is clear that such effects were apparent before this, teachers' use of coursework assessment schemes means that, to an even greater extent, they are faced with an exposition of 'what model of the subject is appropriate', and, furthermore, have overtly to use that model in making judgements about students' work.

In order to ensure that the work produced by students is assessable, teachers must therefore develop and adopt internalised subcultural stances, aligned with the requirements of the assessment scheme being used, whatever their individual pedagogic views. The assessment criteria have to, in a sense, enter the teacher's 'thinking as usual' (Schutz, 1964) so that they are, at least on a day-to-day level, uncontested.[18] (Scarth, 1983) Internalising syllabus requirements in this way will involve different degrees of compromise for different people, but remains necessary for all teachers because of the need to make rapid decisions about assessability during teacher-student and teacher-teacher negotiation. Thus a teacher working on assessed coursework will be dealing simultaneously both with a view of the subject expressed through pedagogic aims, and the internalised, but possibly alternative, subject-based requirements of assessment for a particular syllabus.

Internalised notions of assessability are developed from the teacher's reading of the constraints of the assessment scheme. Such schemes may themselves contain implicit assumptions about what sort of work is assessable, as well as about the nature of assessment. For example, most science assessment schemes are atomistic, giving marks for skills or groups of skills; this is not the case in most other subjects. In the humanities it is generally assumed that the work to be handed in will consist of written accounts, although this is not explicitly stated, and Examining Groups have indicated their willingness to accept work in other forms, such as annotated photographs, if it still indicates that the student has grasped the required concepts.

---

[18] The experience of the Project as a whole is that this internalisation is quite deep, many teachers for example, finding it hard to think outside a mind-set developed in the early years of the GCSE. There is an observed tendency, for example, for teachers to continue to adhere to regulations that have since been lifted, and the cautious interpretations of coursework assesment schemes developed at that time are hard to challenge.

Subject subcultures and coursework 'assessability'

One feature of many subject subcultures is their tendency to develop within teachers a unified or at least dominant view of the nature of their particular subject. The literature in this area rightly stresses that school subject teachers do not form homogeneous subject groups, but that there is debate and contestation between segments within an overall subject group (St.John-Brooks, 1983; Goodson, 1985; Cooper, 1984; 1985a,b; Ball and Lacey, 1980; Ball, 1985). However, the examination syllabus and assessment scheme, superficially, at least, provide a unifying focus for any subcultural grouping, because they lay down a view of what product will result from teachers' classroom work, whatever those teachers' personal stances regarding the nature of their subject. The need to assess means that the teacher has to internalise a view of what counts as, for example, a 'good piece of mathematics', which is particular to the assessment scheme being used. Whatever the teacher's personally developed views about what counts as 'good mathematics', within the context of assessed coursework, what matters is the definition implicit in the assessment scheme.

While, particularly with the post-1994 opening up of the National Curriculum at Key Stage 4, there remains limited freedom of syllabus choice at departmental level, so that a united department is usually able to select a syllabus that reflects at least a broad consensus, teachers as individuals and groups have to adapt themselves to the view of their subject exemplified in the syllabus chosen. This is not always clear-cut, for syllabuses and other curriculum documents are open to interpretation (Ball and Bowe, 1991; Scott, 1990), and the teacher has to be aware not only of the departmental view of an assessment scheme, but also of the view of the moderator, who may see it differently. In negotiating coursework tasks with students and colleagues, teachers have, therefore, constantly to make decisions about the assessability of a piece of work under a particular assessment scheme.

In doing this a number of factors have to be considered. A major concern for some is the sheer amount of coursework that has to be marked:

 There's a member of my department, she teaches sixth form GCSE history and the modules, and sociology as well, and she worked out the other day the amount of pieces of coursework she will have marked, and it is running into thousands. I mean, if you take 200 pupils each producing ten pieces of coursework, then straight away you have two thousand pieces. If you multiply that by the number of modules going on it's an incredible amount.

Paul Barker, head of history, Lacemakers School, 30/1/91

In these circumstances, assessability inevitably includes a requirement that the work should be fairly quick to mark, and there is thus a disincentive to become involved with the sort of projects that require teachers to comb through extended pieces of integrated work, looking for the parts relevant to their subject. Otherwise suitable work that is difficult to mark may thus be ruled out.

Some syllabuses recommend the length of time students are expected to spend on a particular piece of coursework; where work is done with other subjects, teachers may feel that they have to justify the extra time overall that students have been given. For SMP mathematics, for example,

It used to be two to three weeks classroom work, which is now, if you … 1991 handbook says … the 1992 handbook…give the work out four weeks before you want to do it in class, and then after about a month give them two to three weeks classroom time to sort of do it.

Colin Fishbourne, mathematics teacher, Lacemakers School, 17/1/91

This potentially caused problems when students were given a whole term for the mathematics/technology module. However, Colin felt confident that he could justify the time spent by appealing to the fact that much of the work carried out was not mathematically relevant but really design work.

 That's where it's no longer a piece of maths coursework, it's actually technology and this just facilitates. It gives a purpose, if you like, to the module. I mean I don't think you could say, … if I was trying to justify it, if SMP (School Mathematics Project) kick up a fuss, I would say that all the coursework did was give the purpose to the module.

Colin Fishbourne, mathematics teacher, Lacemakers School, 17/1/91

The requirements of the assessment scheme itself may make extra administrative demands on the teacher, leading to a perceived need to limit the possible outcomes of a piece of work. Colin Fishbourne (under pressure from Peter Panther, the deputy head, to do more 'adventurous' work) felt that the need to draw up a marking grid for each task set meant that he had to limit the choice available to the students:

 'It's dead easy to sit in your office and say oh…why can't you do this, why can't you do that….It's something else to get in there and work with the children and then assess it afterwards which is the hardest job there is, you know that. I mean, I've got to go through each of these four tasks and align everything on to there [SMP marking grid, which has to be specifically adapted for each task]. I don't want to do that for these four tasks and do it again in March for the next four.'

Colin Fishbourne, mathematics teacher, Lacemakers School, 2/10/90

The need to show evidence to support one's marking also affected classroom practice, mainly by leading teachers to require students to provide additional supporting material to display the thought processes that they had gone through.

 So my job now is either I think, well, do I leave him, or do I just literally stand there and say, a, b, c, do this, do that, 'cause he's obviously thought about it, but there's no evidence that he's thought about it.

Sally Brightday, Shipbuilders School, 10/1/91

 I mean there's much… the maths coursework requires quite a lot of writing and explaining and communicating and they're sticking with the practical aspects at the moment and I think we'll have to couth that up, you know, the actual body of it.

:

:

:

I'm going to have to really sort of push the write... the last week's going to have to be, well you're going to have to write up the whole thing, if you like, almost like a report.

CP: What, sort of back in the classroom?

Yeah, this is what I have done from the introduction to this and why I did it and why I didn't do it and that's going to have to be more of an input, otherwise it's not going to become valid to the reviewing at the bottom. On that grid there, formulating, communicating, interpreting, that's all got to come through.

Colin Fishbourne, mathematics teacher, Lacemakers School, 2/10/90

Even where there is not a specific requirement that students be able to write about their work, this was sometimes done to provide evidence for moderation. The English teachers at Shipbuilders were particularly anxious about this regarding the children's books project, and asked students to write a 'learning log' to show their thinking as they went along.

 CP: The learning log, is that something you do as a matter of course, or is it special for this project?

It's really special for this project because normally, like the other piece of work they're doing the learning obviously would be evident in the way that they had written it, the input, that would be evident by the way they've finished the piece of work, whereas with the children's project, to my mind just the pictures and very short bits of text, they need some more evidence that they have actually thought about it, because I know that some other teachers do a similar project, they do it in about two weeks time, the kids just write a story, draw some pictures and put it with it, and I want it to be much more than that. I wanted it to be evidence of them thinking, evidence of them negotiating, reflecting on what they've done, reflecting on audience, talking to the kids, all of those things,

Meagan Scanlan, English teacher, Shipbuilders School, 30/4/91

Although Donald Sidcup, the head of department, saw this as simply taking 'the belt and braces approach', Jenny Sims, another English teacher, felt that producing the learning log did not really solve the problem for some students, because it required them to do more of the sort of the work that they were least good at.

 ...a child's story book may look a very simple thing by comparison, with a simple vocabulary and that sort of thing, but because it looks like that doesn't mean that the thought processes behind it's creation are simple at all, and I was amazed by children who I wouldn't normally consider were capable of high level thinking, were actually producing work which showed that there was a high level of thinking. They weren't merely imitating childrens story book style, they were actually able to produce reasoned arguments about why they'd done what they were doing and the effect they felt of what they were doing. So in fact from that point of view there were high levels of thought.

CP: How do you show that for assessment?

It's very difficult. I don't know how you'd show it for assessment. The work can only stand as it stands. I've been them getting to do a learning log, but that's a written piece again and again not all children are capable of that sustained prose.

Jenny Sims, Shipbuilders School, 19/3/91

Conflicts

One of them had said shall we do it like a geographer would, and I said, what do you mean, like a geographer would? You're supposed to be doing this like a thinking person, is a thinking person instantly a geographer, a mathematician or a scientist?

Sarah Cordingley, head of mathematics, Stitchers School, 11/7/91

Unfortunately, for the purposes of assessment, students often have to act like geographers, mathematicians or scientists rather than like 'thinking persons'. Hilary Blondel, the head of special needs at Shipbuilders, found this when she tried to use work in a variety of subjects as part of students' English folders:

The emphasis needed to be different in some things. The child development visit, for example, they have to keep a diary, but the diary is very much directed at certain criteria, so it's a task sheet that they've been given by child development and that didn't actually fit into English. The English sort of diary has to be far more impressions, feelings, whereas the child development one is far more down to looking at particular things, related to child development.

Hilary Blondel, Shipbuilders School, 4/2/91

When departments had to work together directly, the difficulties could be more acute. This was a particular problem with the geography/mathematics/science field course at Stitchers (discussed in more detail in chapter 8). While the geographers needed to be able to assess the way students used their observations, and thus gave the students a lot of help with planning how these were made, the head of mathematics complained that

They do actually still find it extremely difficult to realise that thought processes and planning are part of what we assess and not part of what we tell them to do, and it's not just the facts that we want them to have but also the thought processes. Their whole concept of thought process is completely different.

Sarah Cordingley, Stitchers School, 11/7/91

There were similar problems for the science assessments, exacerbated by the marking scheme, which required teachers to deduct marks from students if they asked for help.

Because, obviously for each assessment category, the more help that you give in that category then... . So it comes to the point where you can do anything for the kids and they'd get no marks for it. The way it has been done before, in the past, no criticism of geography, they need the results, so basically they talk over how to do it, what to do, where to write it down and all the rest of it.

Kevin Simons, science teacher, Stitchers School, 31/10/90

Science assessments are unusual both in this and in the fact that they tend to be rather atomistic in character, marks being awarded for the demonstration of individual skills rather than the design and carrying out of whole experiments. This can be internalised to such an extent that some science teachers find it difficult to work with those from a more holistic tradition. This came out particularly clearly with a proposed media studies/information technology (IT) project at Shipbuilders, where the IT co-ordinator is a scientist. Simon Hastings, the head of media studies, complained that

 I get the feeling anyway, that Rosemary's very scientifically minded and wants to have everything done pat, where...you can see why she's a scientist and you know, and not perhaps an arts teacher in any way, but nobody ...to nail things down like that. It would be impossible for me to work, to start with, I can't work along those lines. I can't see that she helps by having everything nailed to the floor, as far as these little criteria are concerned.., because these little tiny criteria, you know only consist of words, any kind of understanding and translation, you know, Rosemary says, oh we've done that - tick sort of thing, you know, and you think if that's education, you know, then I don't want to know because I don't think that's actually what we're supposed to be doing, there's something other than ticking a box

Simon Hastings, Shipbuilders School, 10/1/91

At the same time, Rosemary complained that she found it difficult to work with Simon, because he was too vague to allow her to do the detailed planning she needed to ensure that the project met the IT assessment criteria (field notes 15/1/90).

Conclusion: increasingly homogeneous subcultures?

Because coursework is, by its very nature, carried out during and as part of the normal learning process, the criteria for its assessment have a far greater influence on pedagogy than does an end-of-course examination. There is usually an expectation that the processes that a student goes through will be assessed, not simply the end outcome, and thus evidence has to be provided for such processes. Furthermore, the greater the percentage of 'normal class work' that is assessed, the more such work has to be screened for assessability at the planning stage. In consequence, when negotiating examination coursework, teachers will tend to impose implicit or explicit constraints, arising out of their perceptions of the assessment scheme, on the students and their work. These will clearly affect discussions between teacher and student, particularly as they may seem arbitrary to the student (or, indeed, the teacher). The discontinuity between the requirements of the assessment scheme and a particular teacher's normal teaching style may be one reason why in many cases coursework does not emerge seamlessly out of normal classwork, as was the original intention of the GCSE. This is especially likely to be the case where there is a conflict between a teacher's subcultural stance regarding pedagogy and the syllabus-based stance regarding assessment, leading assessed work to be seen as somehow different from work focused on learning. Particularly where a teacher feels that the assessment scheme being used imposes tight constraints on what is acceptable, he or she may feel the need to 'signal' to the students that they are being assessed. Many teachers, for example, give students copies of their assessment schemes, in an attempt to ensure that they meet relevant criteria.

Coursework assessment thus has a considerable affect on the ongoing development of subject subcultures, significantly modifying previously held subcultural stances. It is furthermore likely that, with national testing at 7, 11 and 14 and the moves towards uniformity of GCSE examination syllabuses (given not only the requirement that they conform to the National Curriculum but also the considerable reduction in the number on offer overall) assessment will play an increasing rôle in the formation and internalisation of teachers' subcultural stances, combined with decreasing scope for adaptive strategies (avoiding examination classes, using Mode Three courses (Turner, 1983)) on the part of those who do not find it easy to conform to subject norms. As it becomes more apparent that some parts of the National Curriculum are not amenable to testing through examinations and can only be assessed by the teacher as part of longer tasks, the influence of the attainment targets on planning students' work is likely to increase. Indeed, there is already evidence that teachers concentrated on these, rather than the programmes of study, in the first year of the National Curriculum (Her Majesty's Inspectorate, 1991a,b;).

The need to make rapid judgements about whether a proposed piece of work will be 'assessable' requires that the teacher internalise the subject subculture presented in the assessment scheme, alongside her or his (possibly conflicting) personal stance. This will inevitably have a narrowing effect on the range of pedagogic styles that are employed and is likely eventually to result in greater homogeneity of subcultural positions. As the introduction of the National Curriculum brings an increased emphasis on assessment right through compulsory schooling, this issue of assessability as defined by Attainment Targets and Programmes of Study will pervade classroom life to a greater extent than heretofore. Rootedness in an assessment-focused subject subculture is thus likely to be of increased importance to the working lives of teachers.

8 Negotiating Assessed Open Work

In working with schools to develop cross-subject coursework tasks, one of the main concerns of the Project team was to encourage the use of student-centred, open projects, similar to those that were being worked on in design and technology. This was clear in the original funding proposal, which begins:

> This proposal aims to promote and support work by school pupils in which they tackle realistic problems, as part of their learning. In such work, pupils develop personal capability to apply and extend their knowledge and skill, and to exercise responsibility in taking creative decisions, the consequences of which they are then committed to explore.

Project Proposal, June 1988, page 1

There was thus a commitment on the part of the Project team (backed by the interest of the funding agencies) to the development of broad-based open projects. In practice, however, such projects were comparatively rare. This chapter explores some of the reasons why this might have been the case.

For the purposes of this discussion I am regarding an open task as one that leaves some of the decisions to be made regarding the work within or outcomes of that task up to the learner, in negotiation with the teacher (Jones, et al., 1992). However, within the context of coursework being carried out for assessment in a public examination, the notion of openness has to be modified into one of openness within external constraints. While in the normal classroom situation a variety of constraints affect the work carried out, these are likely to be concerned either with such things as available equipment, or with intended learning outcomes, and are in this sense internal to the situation. The additional constraints imposed when work is to be submitted for assessment, on the other hand, may not be concerned with learning at all, but rather with summative assessment and with 'assessability', whether a piece of work is sufficiently aligned with assessment criteria for it to be possible to use those criteria to mark it. The emphasis in planning and carrying out a task thus moves from the processes involved to the end-points to be reached (where such end-points may include having involved a particular set of processes). The ever-present spectre of assessment means that the teacher has always to consider whether the work being carried out, however intrinsically valuable, will also satisfy the assessment scheme.

When negotiating open work in the secondary classroom, a teacher would normally make use of her or his subject subcultural background. This makes it possible to make rapid decisions about a piece of work: whether it is likely to produce outcomes relevant to the subject area; whether it will stretch the student; which knowledge areas are likely to be involved. Because of the nature of the work, open tasks are characterised by frequent but often quite brief negotiations between teacher and students, with the teacher offering advice, some direction, and help where necessary. In most cases this advice will be mediated by the teacher's aims and beliefs about the subject and the role of open work within it; the internalised nature of these allows judgements and decisions to be made rapidly, with little need for prolonged reflection.

Within the context of assessed coursework, the teacher's assessability-related subcultural background is also brought into play. As was stated earlier, an initial expectation of the Project was that a large proportion of the work carried out in schools would consist of open tasks of the kind developed in earlier technology-related projects. This did not in fact occur, and indeed there was often a tendency over time for projects to become less, rather than more, open. This seems to be at least in part a result of the need for teachers to depend on internalised subcultural norms when negotiating work with students in open situations.

Interdisciplinary work in the Project schools took a variety of forms. However, it almost always involved a teacher spending some of his or her time developing work with students that was to be examined in a subject not that teacher's own. In this situation, the teacher does not have the requisite subcultural knowledge necessary for rapid negotiation with students, and it is here that plans for open work can break down. Furthermore, the subcultural norms, particularly regarding the foci and methods of assessment, may not be the same in all subjects, and in some cases can conflict.

Generally, teachers have very little idea of what goes on in other subjects. Even where there has been extensive curriculum audit, or where teachers have read each other's syllabuses, there is little understanding of what 'covering' a particular topic in another subject really means. There is a particular failure to allow for progression in subjects that are not a teacher's own, so that while it may be recognised that a piece of work is likely to involve another area, the level (from the point of view of the other subject) of such work is often not considered.[19] This was one of the issues that stimulated the art and English departments at Shipbuilders to start to work more closely together. Both departments had already carried out projects involving students writing and illustrating children's books, but when they compared results, they found that their understandings of what students could do were often unrealistic and that simultaneous academic under-expectation and volume over-expectation had taken place.

 I mean, one of the problems that was coming up for the first time in the English department...they had books that they were very pleased with, because obviously they were looking at them from a literature point of view, and when they actually flashed them at us for an artistic point of view, they were a bit disappointed because we didn't seem thrilled to bits. You know, we have similar problems the other way. We have shown them books that we thought the graphics were great on and they have read the stories and put their head in their hands and said, "I don't believe this is happening."

Sally Brightday, head of art, Shipbuilders School, 6/11/90

---

[19] This is likely to be a particular problem for information technology (IT) when it is taught and assessed across the curriculum. Teachers find it dificult to relate progression in IT to progression in their own subjects. While they may include IT work within the curriculum, they are likely to find it difficult to develop students' understanding of IT in the same way as they do that of their subject and thus to have a clear idea of differentiation when it comes to assessment.

Originally, English teachers were sort of asking them to illustrate everything, which is ridiculous, whereas in fact, you know, Sally, the head of art was saying, you're not really, you're talking about one or two things...so we as English teachers were actually asking something very unrealistic of our students, and in terms of GCSE, you know, one of the original criticisms was overload for the students. It was our ignorance as English teachers, it was very well intended, but we didn't realise what we were asking the kids to do. Now the fact that we've got this tie-up for teachers, and the fact that we've actually got down to discuss it, what we were asking them to do, has made it easier for the kids.

Donald Sidcup, head of English, Shipbuilders School, 4/2/91

Emphases in subjects may also vary. In mathematics, for example, it is considered important for students to have a clear understanding of the processes involved in mathematical operations, and it is this that is assessed as much as the successful carrying out of those operations per se. This was a cause of misunderstandings at Stitchers, where Stephen Fieldwork, the head of geography, believed that he did a lot of mathematics work, although this often consisted of substitution of figures into worked examples done on the board; this was not acceptable for mathematics assessment. English teachers similarly feel the need to take care that work done in other subjects and submitted for English is 'original' in the English sense of the term.

One of the problems about a lot of work from any other subject is, from an English point of view, its too derivative. It may well meet the requirements of say science or humanities but for a piece of English work, its often very dull, very boring, totally unoriginal and yes they may have demonstrated the scientific or humanities concepts, but as a piece of English it is not particularly interesting, or worthwhile and it will get poor grades.

Donald Sidcup, head of English, Shipbuilders School, 6/11/90

Working in a cross-curricular way can challenge subculturally-based assumptions and lead to unease. Colin Fishbourne, the mathematics teacher supporting the technology module at Lacemakers, had in effect to relinquish the responsibility for the negotiation and production of mathematics coursework to a teacher of another subject. This caused him some anxiety when the norms of his subject ran up against the different expectations of the CDT teacher.

... he's much more used to long projects and things taking a long time and I've never been involved in a piece of work that's taken four weeks before, really. I mean if we set one of these in a maths lesson it'll have to be done in four weeks, and then we say finito, signed, sealed, delivered, here you go, and he's not worried if they're only on their second drawing or whatever, and I'm a bit more...I want to see it getting somewhere...I'd rather see it coming together quicker than it is...I mean, I hope it'll come together in the end.

Colin Fishbourne, Lacemakers School, 2/10/90

A teacher negotiating open coursework within one subject area has as a main concern the assessability of that coursework, and in particular the boundaries of subject matter, approach and teacher input implicit in marking schemes. These can be difficult to convey to teachers of other subjects, however well-intentioned, because words have subtly different shades of meaning between one subject and another, and what counts as unacceptable help in one subject may be seen as normal practice in another. For example, many teachers see the practice of re-drafting in English as a form of cheating, of unfair enhancement of students' work, whereas it is considered by English teachers and examiners as normal good practice. English teachers, on the other hand, are apt to consider students' work using quotation from reference sources as 'not their own work' and therefore unacceptable. Beliefs about the amount of work involved in assessing work from different subjects can also lead to resistance to collaboration if it is felt that it will lead to an inequitable marking load.

 I think that is one of the problems that humanities people by and large understand, differentiated marking, they understand coursework, they understand objectives etc. Whereas non humanities people don't. I'm not saying they couldn't, but they just don't understand that setting a piece of coursework is not a straightforward thing, and a mark scheme maybe needs four or five levels of answer for each question.

:

:

:

it's not marking as maybe mathematicians or physicists think about, it's marking as humanities people think about, which is again, a totally different ball game. I mean differentiated answers and questions.

Paul Barker, head of humanities, Lacemakers School, 30/1/91

Such variations in perceptions of the openness of coursework for other subjects is a major source of misunderstanding between teachers.

Intersections between subcultures: misunderstandings and manoeverings at Stitchers School

The kinds of difficulties that can arise when subject subcultures rub up against each other in open tasks can be illustrated by the experience of the teachers working on the geography/mathematics/science field course at Stitchers school. Although other factors were of course involved, it is clear that the subcultural givens of the various subjects, and in particular the degree of task openness assumed by both the teachers and their assessment schemes, caused considerable problems in the design, carrying out and assessment of the joint tasks.

The joint field course took place twice during the time that I was involved in the school, once before the more detailed study started (1990) and once towards the end of it (1991). I was therefore able to interview some of the key actors as they moved from reflecting on their experiences in the first year of its operation towards planning and carrying out their second attempt. The staff centrally involved in both the planning and operation of the field course were the head of geography, Stephen Fieldwork, Jeremy Paxton, a member of his department, the head of mathematics, Sarah Cordingley, and the head of integrated science, Kevin Simons. Two other teachers also took part in the course but were not involved in joint coursework. I interviewed all four 'central' staff as well as a number of students, after the first run through, and all staff except Jeremy Paxton during the planning of the second attempt. Kevin Simons and Sarah Cordingley were also interviewed after the second run through; I was, however, unable to re-interview Stephen Fieldwork or Jeremy Paxton at this stage due to their absence on other field courses (both subsequently left the school at the end of the year). I was also unable to talk with any students who took part in the course the second time around. It must be appreciated, then, that this account is both partial and biased towards the views of the mathematics and science teachers involved. It is nevertheless illustrative of the sort of subcultural conflicts that may arise and the lengths to which teachers will go to resolve or to side-step them.

The underlying issue between the departments involved was the degree of openness of the tasks that the students had to carry out. There were also problems concerning the assumptions that the various teachers held about each other's subjects; these revolved around the importance of the assessment of processes. Over the course of the study, it became increasingly clear that these were fundamental issues that the teachers found it difficult to resolve, or indeed to explain to each other; each individual's beliefs were so rooted in their subject subculture that they seemed the only way for things to be. Consequently they found it difficult to get them across to others, and at times there appeared to be points of mutual understanding that were not subsequently borne out in practice. This eventually led to some acrimony and attempts to manipulate the situation to enable particular subject aims to be achieved.

These events were also played out against a background of power inequalities and, eventually, mutual mistrust. The field course was originally geography only and the geography department still carried out all the administration of it (other teachers complained that they were kept uninformed about what was happening). Only students studying geography took part in the course, and they generally referred to it as a 'geography trip'; several, furthermore, expressed resentment at what they saw as a takeover by science, which had led to them having to do much more work than they had expected. The geography department was very proud of their examination success; they got the best results in the school (Graham Peacock, field notes, 16/1/91) and had a large number of 'A' level students. This made them understandably resistant to any change that might jeopardise their position. Meanwhile, the heads of both mathematics and science told me on separate occasions that it was easier to do well in geography than in their subjects because it was 'less rigorous' (field notes 27/9/90 and 4/12/90). Sarah Cordingley also believed that the emphases of her department were more conducive to student learning; she was therefore interested in changing geography department practices for what she perceived as sound educational reasons.

 ...we've got to get them to realise that the children can't produce such immaculate work, if we actually want it to be *better*.

Sarah Cordingley, 11/7/91

The key point of conflict was, essentially, the aims and purposes of the field course, particularly for the two departments that had the greatest stake in it, geography and science. For the geographers, the emphasis was on students observing landforms for themselves and on the taking of accurate measurements to test a variety of hypotheses given to the students by the department. Accuracy of data was important, as it needed to be pooled between all those in the group, and because the department was concerned that students should come to conclusions that would enhance their geographical understanding. While it was important that the students tested the hypotheses themselves, it was crucial that the results be accurate; this was seen taking precedence over the processes gone through in obtaining them. For the science department, on the other hand, it was the reverse. They wanted to assess students' practical skills in the field; the way that they went about the experiments and how they dealt with problems and experimental failure was far more critical for this than the results they got. The two departments were thus aiming at making assessments that would often be mutually incompatible. This was exacerbated by a science marking scheme that required teachers to reduce the marks given to students who asked for help.

Because, obviously for each assessment category, the more help that you give in that category then... right. So it comes to the point where you can do anything for the kids and they'd get no marks for it. The way it has been done before, in the past, no criticism of geography, they need the results, so basically they talk over how to do it, what to do, where to write it down and all the rest of it.

:

:

:

Out of the four categories, just off the top of my head, category A is using apparatus, so what basically you do is, if they have a device which they have chosen to use, then they can sort of follow a set of instructions and can use it adequately. Well that was OK apart from the fact that when it was found that one or two of the pupils couldn't do as they were told, couldn't follow the instructions they were given...instead of assistance being given to them, what would happen is that a member of staff will go over and do it for them, give them the reading, and then they would, you know, and immediately you see they have absolutely destroyed it. For category B, again off the top of my head, I think that is making measurements and observations, which is fine if the member of staff stays out of the way and allows them to make the measurements or whatever, and then can at the end say 'well I don't think you were being accurate enough, do you not think you ought to do it or... ' Something like that, or possibly even if for geography they can take the measurements themselves and say, well, this is what you should have got, and how close you got to it, and done it that way, but it wasn't, again.

Drawing conclusions - what conclusions were given to them, this is the next category, C. Conclusions were given to them before they got anywhere near to thinking about what their results were like, and it was just an end of day debrief, just, 'this is what you should have found', and they're thinking well, you know, basically we've just not done that.

The design one was OK, because I did a lot of that before we went away, it got me thinking about what we would be able to do. But again what happened was that in order to get the maximum six, they need to get across some sort of problem and change their design. Now what happened was when they came across the problems and you know, various different things they needed to, they couldn't quite get it. Instead of allowing them to sit down and redesign and evaluate what they had done, a member of staff would plough straight in and say don't do that, do it like this. It's understandable, because geography need the results and they're not interested in the way in which they're got, but it detracts from the science.

Kevin Simons, 31/10/90

If I am going to compare, lets shall we say ... discharges at a particular site ... I need to know that there is consistency of measurement there. Science on the other hand may be looking for how can you...having measured at one site...one location...[...]... How can we improve it ... right lets go ... the same location site two - how do we improve it...[...]...Now that's fine as long as they can then ensure that the information I want collected is collected. What I can't do is turn round and say , OK, science, we will use yours ... oh what a pity ...

Stephen Fieldwork, 31/10/90

As a result of these incompatibilities, which only became apparent when they were in the field[20], the first time the joint project was attempted the geography department inadvertently invalidated many of the science assessments.

Although at this level the teachers involved were able to perceive their differences quite clearly, the process of negotiating changes for the following year brought deeper subcultural incompatibilities to the fore. It was at this point that some of the terms common to the various subjects turned out to mean different things to different people; this was again connected with varying degrees of openness in the work. This led to continued problems in the second year of the project.

 ...for Assessment D, which is their planning. The only part of that which sort of caused a lot of headaches beforehand was that to get a maximum six for that skill, they have to evaluate what they have done. Now my statements were, that if they are going to evaluate it, then they have to go through the learning procedure of realising that they have done something wrong, that they could have done something better. Geography's arguments were, well they've planned it, if we tell them how to do it perfectly, surely they can evaluate it in the light of the perfect way to do it; and again it reached the situation where I was banging my head against a brick wall, and I said right, we'll do the design, I'll part mark it on the design, get them to do it their way first of all and then you can do it the perfect way, and we'll see what happens in the evaluation. Now some of the evaluations I am sure are going to be written up that 'my way was not very good, geography's way was much better'. In which case, I mean, that virtually worthless, in that they haven't gone through the realisation process.

Kevin Simons, 11/7/91

The sort of evaluation needed by the science department remained incompatible with geography's need for accuracy, and all that was possible was an uneasy truce.

The pressure on the geographers was exacerbated by Sarah Cordingley's desire to get more mathematics out of the activity than she had done in the first year, when it was realised too late that the geography department had controlled students' work too closely for it to be assessable as practical mathematics, which has an emphasis on open tasks. There was an additional need to re-negotiate the mathematics/geography link: the geographers were making increased use of computer packages that did for them most of the mathematics that she had hoped to assess before. For Sarah, the key issue was that students should devise their own methods of measuring, recording and writing up.

---

[20] or, to be more accurate, waist-deep in a river in the rain

She was also trained to teach science, and so tended to line up with the science department when negotiations became difficult. Resistance by the geographers to pressure from two more powerful departments led to a certain amount of mutual distrust, which did not make negotiations any easier. As Sarah Cordingley put it:

 I mean I don't know how much help they will give and how much support, and they may not always, you know, tell me the truth about what they do in their classroom. But I can't actually go round and monitor every single classroom.

Sarah Cordingley, 17/5/91

This distrust was to some extent justified, as emerged in the student interviews:

 [for science] You had to decide what experiment you were going to do; instead of being told you had to do that experiment, you had to figure it out for yourself kind of thing.

CP: Did you find that the geography teacher sort of got in the way of that by telling you the experiment to do?

Yes. Before we went, um, Mr Paxton told us what we was doing but he said don't tell Mr Simons that he'd told us. Yes, because he wanted to make it as simple as possible but Mr Simons just sort of said, right you make a test and see if its true, and we were a bit confused about that because we didn't know how to go about it.

But we sort of knew what to do because Mr. Paxton had explained it before we went.

CP: So Mr Simons told you to make a test but you'd been told what test to do already?

(laughing) Yeah, he said, don't say anything otherwise I'll get done.

Stitchers Year 11 students, 31/10/90

By the time the joint project was carried out for the second time, all the staff concerned had become frustrated by the failure of their protracted negotiations to resolve all the problems and misunderstandings. In the event, Kevin Simons was unable to go on the trip for family reasons, so Sarah Cordingley was accompanied by another member of her own department and took on the responsibility for ensuring that the science work was carried out in such a way as to be assessable. By this stage she saw her rôle as preventing the geography department from closing off the tasks, by whatever means possible. This is her account of how she did this:

 I actually went in when Stephen explained it. That didn't go down too well either, because he wanted me to go away or go out for the evening or something, and I didn't. I sat down with the children and said I was just going to take a few notes....That didn't sit extremely well.

CP: You mean you made sure you were present at the time?

I made sure that there was no formalised recording system given to the children.

:

:

:

We each had two groups. Ours had a little more freedom, some of theirs they actually told them to 'write a table like this'. Well that was easy. We got them back that night, I took over the section, and I went round and said, I've seen this table, sixteen times before. Do you think you're going to really get high marks if you present your results in this fashion?

CP: So you actually went round and undermined what they'd done?

I went round and did a fair bit of, what would you get in Maths from Mr Palmer? What would you get in Maths from Mr Conway? Suppose I was marking this?
Sarah Cordingley, 11/7/91

In this way she ensured that the work produced was assessable for mathematics and science; it is unclear (and I was unable to ask the people concerned) whether she consequently made it difficult or impossible to assess it for geography.

Some suggestions

Teachers are acutely aware of the gap between others' perceptions of their subject and their own, and in particular of the differences between subjects regarding what is acceptable for assessment. They are also aware of the scope for misunderstandings such as those apparent in the negotiations at Stitchers, and the attendant possibilities for invalidating each other's work. Consequently, when cross-curricular projects are being conceived, there is an enormous temptation to 'tie everything down' in such a way that no-one can misunderstand. This tendency to get everything into what one teacher called 'tidy-boxes' works directly against the development of open work, as teachers attempt to control all the possible outcomes so that their colleagues are unable to let them down, or vice versa.

The difficulties for the planning and carrying out of tasks involving multiply assessed open coursework tasks arise from the overlap of complexities in all the different components. The negotiation of open work is in itself complex and relies to a large extent on ongoing, subculturally rooted judgements on the part of the teacher. If such work is to be assessed, a further subcultural layer is introduced, with the teacher having to bear in mind not only pedagogic considerations but also notions of assessability implicit in an interpretation of the criteria for assessment. If the intention of dual accreditation is introduced to this already complex scene, requiring teachers to work within the subcultural norms underlying the assessment of subjects other than their own, the whole project can collapse.

At this point the tendency has been for teachers to move away from open work towards coursework tasks that are much more constrained. However, this is not necessarily the best way forward. A partial solution being developed in some schools is the abandonment of dual accreditation while still carrying out joint tasks. One area where this has been successful is in work done in or around design and technology (d&t) subjects. Most D&T courses require a long individual project, and schools have found that the length of this task and its position late in the course makes it difficult to use as the basis of joint coursework. However, it is unusual for students not to have carried out other similar but shorter projects earlier in the course, and these can be set up in such a way that they provide or contribute to coursework tasks for another subject. At Lacemakers, students taking design and communication produced a piece of mathematics coursework this way. Lacemakers also made use of an area not normally assessed, developing integrated humanities work from PSE (personal and social education). Although this threatened to run into problems because those teaching PSE were by and large not humanities teachers, and the head of department expressed concerns about standardisation of marking, the moderator considered the work produced through PSE to be some of the best in the course.

Timetable manipulations can also be a way to ensure that all relevant subcultural assumptions are catered for. These can take a number of forms, and some are more successful than others. Timetable suspension, which has been tried in several schools, can in fact exacerbate the problems, as students tend to end up working with only one or two teachers throughout, and have less access than usual to teachers of the other subjects involved. The tendency in this kind of project for teachers to take students off-site and to work through the lunch hour means that staff are also less accessible to each other and so tend to carry on without consultation once the project has begun; this makes it more likely that teachers, basing their judgements on subculturally-based misunderstandings, will inadvertently invalidate each other's work.

Team-teaching has been more successful, both where one teacher has major responsibility for the group and is occasionally supported by the other, and where two teachers work together with a double-size group, such as the combined arts course at Lacemakers. In the technology module at the same school, it was noticed that students tended to save mathematical queries for the days when the mathematics teacher was present, and were encouraged to do so by the CDT specialist who did most of the teaching. This system also ensured that the students recorded their work in such a way that it could relatively easily be assessed for mathematics. Where it has not been possible to put two teachers in one classroom, even once a week, time has sometimes been given to the teachers involved in a project to meet on a regular basis while it is going on so that they are able to share ideas and pick up any problems arising at an early stage; this did, however, happen at Stitchers, suggesting that even then some difficulties may remain intractable. Generally, however, where joint coursework has broken down it has tended to be in cases where while there was initial discussion, this was not continued while the work was being carried out. Close and continued communication, however informal, is essential. This is the case even with closed interdisciplinary tasks, but is especially so with regard to open work.

If openness is to be preserved in cross-curricular coursework, teachers need time to discuss in detail the nature of their various subjects, as well as the particular requirements of the planned task, in terms of both pedagogy and assessability. In this way, it may be possible to convey to others key points at which it is important to ensure that advice it obtained from the subject specialist. In coming to this process, teachers will need to abandon their preconceptions of others' subjects, particularly those bound up with subject status, so that the central issues for all concerned can be made clear. This is not as easy as one might at first imagine. A little knowledge can indeed be a dangerous thing, and it is essential that teachers come to this process in a spirit of respect for the mores of each others' subjects. One teacher described in this way the essential quality that he saw as necessary for good co-operation:

 you have got to have people who are generous...you can't legislate for that generosity, you know, you can't actually put it down on the application form and say, 'you must be a generous person', but that is what is needed, and if it isn't there it does become difficult.

Martin Morton, assistant deputy curriculum, Lacemakers School, 12/11/90

9 | Conclusions and Implications

 So I think it's been a successful year. I think it has. I think every year is...we move a bit really. We leave a bit. It's like a sort of tide that shifts the debris a little bit further every time. Yeah, I think we have made progress.

Peter Panther, deputy head, Lacemakers School, 2/7/91

Why is it that teachers find assessed interdisciplinary work so hard? And why, despite this, do they persist in trying to achieve and improve it? The answers to these questions are of course complex, and I do not claim to have arrived at them. However, in this book I have explored a number of factors, some common to innovation in general, others to do with cross-curricular work in particular. Both have been considered, because it is the added dimension of working across subjects on tasks whose outcomes will be subjected to the rigours of assessment that brings out and clarifies what is involved in school-based curriculum development. When teachers of different subjects come together to plan coursework that will be carried out jointly, this points up issues in innovatory practice that would normally be hidden; it is these that have been the subject of this book. It is now time to draw the strands together and consider the implications.

Curriculum Issues

A key issue in all of this is the concept of subject subculture. Most of the difficulties coming out of the development of interdisciplinary coursework stem in some part from subcultural clashes and incompatibilities. This is not to say that the problems ordinarily encountered during school-based innovation all come down to subcultural issues; it is rather that part of the rôle of the subject culture is to draw teachers together within subject groups and thus to smooth over what might otherwise be intractable differences. Because the subject culture is such a central part of a subject teacher's 'thinking as usual', it forms a generally understood 'normality' through which individual agendas are addressed and to which ambitions and attempts at change are related. Even while the culture is contested, that contestation centres around a broader agreed sense of the subject; it can still be distinguished from other curriculum areas by practitioners and others. Furthermore, even if individuals disagree with the dominant view, they are still able to recognise the (current) centrality of that view, and adjust their behaviour accordingly; ambitious teachers will go along with ideas that they disagree with, if only to rise to positions where they may be able to influence the majority opinion.

When working across the curriculum, however, such understandings are not common, and teachers find it harder to locate themselves in the more generally contested school culture. Their micropolitical moves become more obvious and conflicts more apparent. Difficulties that would otherwise be accommodated loom larger and may appear intractable. At the same time, without the backdrop of mutual understanding that characterises single-subject curriculum negotiation, there is a much greater likelihood of clashes in interpretations and intentions. Differences within cultures can no longer be subsumed into the need to conform to the dominant (assessment-influenced) view, while differences between cultures gain added importance when they form a barrier to communication. Furthermore, because most teachers' previous experience has been entirely within the confines of a particular subject, much that is arbitrary (such as the precise meanings of technical terms, particularly those that have alternative definitions outside the classroom context) is seen as uncontested and given; it may therefore be some time before teachers realise that they are talking at cross purposes. Many differences may also be hidden by ambiguity. In the meantime, failure to conform to expectations (such as the provision of the precise degree of openness required by a particular subject's definition of 'investigation') leads to confusion and mistrust.

Related assessment issues

Mutual misunderstandings cannot on their own explain, however, why teachers find cross-subject projects so difficult to design, carry out, and, in particular, to assess. The Project was originally set up because of the need to assess cross-subject work for GCSE. We realised early on, however, that the mechanisms and procedures of the Examining Groups were not an issue, but that teachers nevertheless perceived the assessment of interdisciplinary work as being fraught with problems. In part this was simply a question of publicity management; when the Examining Groups lifted their restrictions on the multiple accreditation of coursework this was usually announced in their general regulations, rather than in the individual syllabuses that classroom teachers read. However, even when the logistical wrinkles were ironed out, it was still apparent that designing interdisciplinary coursework in such a way that it could be assessed for the contributing subjects was a more complex task than at first appeared. This is again linked to the influence of and teachers' identification with, subject subcultures. In particular, it is connected with the ways in which ideas of assessability are embedded in subject subcultural understandings, to the extent that they are used almost subconsciously.

In preparing and carrying out work in their 'home' subject, teachers automatically consider how evidence for attainment will be produced; a view of what will satisfy the assessment scheme at any particular level is a part of the teacher's thinking-as-usual in understanding what the subject is about. Even though the National Curriculum forced teachers to approach assessment in a particular and often novel way, the conception of the nature of the various subjects remained largely unchanged. Except where, as in design and technology and AT1 in mathematics and science, there was the intention to develop all or part of a new curriculum area, the content and processes embodied in the programmes of study and attainment targets were largely based on what was seen as best practice at the time. Because assessment schemes have such a pervasive (and increasing) influence on subject cultures, notions of assessability underlie all of a teacher's beliefs about what constitutes a particular subject and what is appropriate work for students to do. This not only means that virtually everything that is done is automatically assessable, it also makes it comparatively easy for teachers to recognise 'assessment opportunities' when they occur in their classrooms. Assessment itself is unproblematic; it is the recording, collation and providing evidence for assessment decisions that needs to be sorted out.

When working across the curriculum, however, teachers are no longer embedded in a subject culture that is in part founded on criteria of assessability. Nor do they carry in their heads such a deeply understood idea of what they might see that would constitute evidence for crediting a student with a particular level of attainment. It is therefore necessary when planning interdisciplinary work to build in such understandings explicitly from the start, so that teachers of all the subjects involved are able to ensure that the work produced can be assessed, and that they will recognise achievement when it is demonstrated. For this to happen, however, entails a change both in teachers' thinking about assessment and in their practice of it.

Because teachers have embedded subcultural understandings of what will count as recordable achievement, approaching the assessment of single-subject work as if it were simply a question of finding a good recording system has generally been a successful strategy. The influence of assessment on the subject subculture means that when they come to recording, teachers are not faced with systems that fail to correspond to the work the students produce. This success has naturally led teachers to carry this approach over to cross-curricular projects. Plans for assessment have thus focused on the need for efficient recording systems and little attention has been paid to how one will recognise what is to be recorded, or even how one will ensure that there is anything to record. Schools have devised elaborate audit schemes that note, for example, where students encounter information technology applications, but which fail to help teachers to develop progression or recognise differentiation in the subject; both formative and summative assessment are tackled too late.

Bringing it all together

It is therefore essential in planning interdisciplinary work, even more than as part of innovation in general, that teachers be given time to explore the nature of the work proposed and the hopes and expectations that they bring to it. Space must be provided not just for planning, but also for the exploration of meanings, so that, even if it is impossible to come to mutual understandings, at least there is an acknowledgement of differences. Such acknowledgement should include an awareness that people bring a variety of agendas to any situation and that these may not all be ones that school management would normally consider 'legitimate'. Institutional reasons for undertaking particular innovations should also be clearly articulated, so that teachers can orient themselves in relation to these. There may also be a role here for the sensitive use of teacher appraisal systems as part of making space for teachers' personal and career agendas overtly to be recognised and valued. The multiplicity of reasons that people have for doing things need not be a barrier to successful innovation. Carrying on as if everyone had the same motives, however, is likely to lead to dissatisfaction on the part of those whose agendas are not being addressed, with consequent failure of commitment. In particular, it is essential to recognise that agreement about the action to be taken does not necessarily imply agreement about the reasons for that action. Unless such reasons are explored and made explicit, there is likely to be a breakdown in activity if the planned course of action needs to be changed once a project is under way.

Even when interdisciplinary negotiation runs smoothly, teachers still do not have access to each other's implicit subcultural understandings of progression and differentiation. Consequently, when work is planned, assessment frameworks do not get built in automatically, and have to be specifically considered. It is not assessment itself that is the problem, nor is it the recording of assessment, even across several subjects. What is at issue is the perception by teachers and managers that what they need is a complex recording system, when in fact by the time they get to recording it may be too late. A change of approach is needed, from planning based on subcultural understandings with assessment and assessability more or less taken for granted, to an realisation that, in the cross-disciplinary context, there is need to find ways of designing activities so that assessment opportunities and assessable work will come out of them. Teachers find interdisciplinary assessment difficult because they are tackling the wrong issue. We must stop searching for all-purpose assessment systems and find some way of helping people to realise that when we approach interdisciplinary work we are doing something much more new than at first appears.

There is also a need for explicitness in the processes of decision making and taking. It has to be recognised at all levels that authority in decision taking and responsibility for the outcomes of decisions taken go hand in hand; if teachers are not given the authority they are likely to refuse the responsibility. This authority should usually extend to the framing as well as the resolution of issues to be decided; if this does not happen there may well be a feeling that the important decisions (as epitomised by the problem frame) have been taken elsewhere, and that it is there that responsibility should lie. Work also needs to be done with both teachers and school managers on the generation of alternative problem frames, so that a wider range of possible solutions may be arrived at. If this does not occur, management-framed decisions will be restricted to what is deemed possible by the thinking-as-usual of the management subculture. By framing issues comparatively openly in advance of discussion, school managers can, on the other hand, be proactive in opening up the possibility of more creative approaches to curriculum planning.

The way forward

With the reduction in the compulsory curriculum as a result of the Dearing proposals (Dearing, 1994), there is renewed scope for working towards the greater integration of school subjects. A period of curricular stability coupled with greater freedom at Key Stage 4 provide both an opportunity and a challenge to schools wanting to give their students a diet that is both rich and appropriate. Increased choice at Key Stage 4 is a mixed blessing, and many schools will want to ensure that all students still study a broad and balanced curriculum, while making space for specialised interests. Interdisciplinary work can play an important part in this, either by allowing more to be fitted into what remains a crowded timetable, or by opening up a range of ways by which short courses, whether compulsory or optional, can be assessed. There is also the challenge of vocational education, and how it is to be fitted into both the timetable and the assessment process. Cross-subject work provides one approach to this, which among other advantages, would allow all students to have a vocational component in their GCSE courses, without having to forgo the option of doing academic work beyond the core.

Assessed cross-curricular work is difficult but worthwhile. It allows students to pursue projects that have more relevance to the interdisciplinary world 'out there', and which may have a closer correspondence to their present and future concerns. It offers a possible way of introducing a vocational element to academic courses, and vice versa. Among teachers, it can promote a deeper understanding of the learning process, as methodologies are compared across subjects. Well planned, it can save students time and allow them to carry out longer, more open and more substantial tasks. As a way of dealing with a crowded curriculum, it offers many advantages.

To achieve this entails an understanding that interdisciplinary work, particularly when it has to be assessed, requires a radically different approach to that common in single-subject planning. The importance of the subject culture in designing assessable work must be fully taken on board in working towards cross-curricular approaches to schooling. If this does not occur, teachers will continue to design projects which, however interesting they are to carry out, may not lead to assessable outcomes. Working on cross-subject projects with assessment firmly in mind from the start forces teachers to make some of their implicit assumptions explicit, enabling them to integrate better their curriculum and assessment thinking. Such insights should feed back profitably into single-subject work as well as making interdisciplinary projects run more smoothly.

The opening up of the curriculum at Key Stage 4 provides us with a new challenge. Well-planned, assessable interdisciplinary work has a major part to play in the future curriculum. It is important that this opportunity not be missed because of planning that does not take into account the particular issues involved. In clarifying and exploring these, this book is intended to help all those concerned to provide a relevant and dynamic education for our students. But for changes to take place in practice, a lot of work needs to be done in schools; this will require time, effort and self-examination. It is to be hoped that teachers, managers and students will feel able to rise to the challenge.

References

Ball, S.J. (1985) 'English for the English since 1906', in: I. F. Goodson (Ed) *Social Histories of the Secondary Curriculum* (Lewes, Falmer Press).

Ball, S.J. (1987) *The micropolitics of the school* (London, Methuen).

Ball, S.J. and Bowe, R. (1992) Subject departments and the 'implementation' of National Curriculum policy: an overview of the issues, *Journal of Curriculum Studies*, 24:2, pp 97-115.

Ball, S.J. and Lacey, C. (1980) 'Subject disciplines as the opportunity for group action: a measured critique of subject subcultures', in: P. Woods (Ed) *Teacher Strategies* (London, Croom Helm).

Barnes, D. and Seed, J. (1984) 'Seals of approval: an analysis of English examinations', in: I. F. Goodson and S. J. Ball (Eds) *Defining the Curriculum: Histories and Ethnographies* (Lewes, Falmer Press).

Brown, P. (1987) *Schooling Ordinary Kids* (London, Tavistock Press).

Brown, S.I. and Walter, M. (1983) *The Art of Problem Posing* (New Jersey, Lawrence Erlbaum Associates.).

Cooper, B. (1984) 'On explaining change in school subjects', in: I. F. Goodson and S. J. Ball (Eds) *Defining the Curriculum: Histories and Ethnographies* (Lewes, Falmer Press).

Cooper, B. (1985a) 'Secondary school mathematics since 1950: reconstructing differentiation', in: I. F. Goodson (Ed) *Social Histories of the Secondary Curriculum* (Lewes, Falmer Press).

Cooper, B. (1985b) *Renegotiating Secondary School Mathematics* (Lewes, Falmer Press).

Dearing, R. (1994) *The National Curriculum and its Assessment* (London, School Curriculum and Assessment Authority).

Fullan, M.G. (1982) *The Meaning of Educational Change* (New York/Ontario, Teachers' College Press/OISE Press).

Fullan, M.G. (1991) *The New Meaning of Educational Change* (London, Cassell Educational).

Goodson, I.F. (1985) 'Subjects for study', in: I. F. Goodson (Ed) *Social Histories of the Secondary Curriculum* (Lewes, Falmer Press).

Handy, C.B. (1985) *Understanding Organizations Third Edition* (Harmondsworth, Middlesex, Penguin Books).

Handy, C.B. and Aitken, R. (1986) *Understanding Schools as Organizations* (London, Penguin Books).

Her Majesty's Inspectorate (1991a) *Mathematics at Key Stages 1 and 3: A Report by HM Inspectorate of the 1st Year 1989-90* (London, HMSO).

Her Majesty's Inspectorate (1991b) *Science at Key Stages 1 and 3: A Report by HM Inspectorate of the 1st Year 1989-90* (London, HMSO).

Jones, A.T., Simon, S.A., Black, P.J., Fairbrother, R.W. and Watson, J.R. (1992) *Open Work in Science: development of investigations in schools* (Hatfield, Association for Science Education).

MacDonald, B. and Walker, R. (1976) *Changing the Curriculum* (London, Open Books).

Marris, P. (1975) *Loss and Change* (New York, Anchor Press/Doubleday).

Marsh, C., Day, C., Hannay, C. and McCutcheon, G. (1990) *Reconceptualising School-Based Curriculum Development* (Basingstoke, Falmer Press).

Murray, R., with Paechter, C.F. and Black, P.J. (1994) *Managing Learning and Assessment Across the Curriculum* (London, Her Majesty's Stationery Office).

National Curriculum Council (1989a) *Mathematics: Non-Statutory Guidance* (York, National Curriculum Council).

National Curriculum Council (1989b) *Science: Non-Statutory Guidance* (York, National Curriculum Council).

National Curriculum Council (1990a) *Non-Statutory Guidance: Information Technology Capability* (York, National Curriculum Council).

National Curriculum Council (1990b) *Technology in the National Curriculum* (London, Her Majesty's Stationery Office).

Paechter, C.F. (1995) Subcultural Retreat: negotiating the Design and Technology Curriculum, *British Educational Research Journal*, 21: 1 pp. 75 – 87.

Popkewitz, T.S. (1984) *Paradigm and Ideology in Educational Research* (Lewes, Falmer Press).

Redway, K. (1992) *Managing Change: seminar notes* (London, Kathryn Redway Associates).

Reid, W.A. (1984) 'Curricular topics as institutional categories: implications for theory and research in the history and sociology of school subjects', in: I. F. Goodson and S. J. Ball (Eds) *Defining the Curriculum: Histories and Ethnographies* (Lewes, Falmer Press).

Ruddock, J. (1991) *Innovation and Change* (Buckingham, Open University Press).

Sarason, S. (1982) *The Culture of the School and the Problem of Change (revised edition)* (Boston, Allyn and Bacon).

Scarth, J. (1983) 'Teachers' school-based experience of examining', in: M. Hammersley and A. Hargreaves (Eds) *Curriculum Practice: Some Sociological Case Studies* (Lewes, Falmer Press).

Schutz, A. (1964) 'The stranger', in: B. R. Cosin, I. R. Dale, G. M. Esland, D. MacKinnon and D. F. Swift (Eds) *School and Society* (London, Routledge and Kegan Paul).

Scott, D. (1990) *Coursework and Coursework Assessment in the GCSE: CEDAR Report 6* (Warwick, University of Warwick).

Smith, L.M. and Keith, P.M. (1971) *Anatomy of Educational Innovation: an Organizational Analysis of an Elementary School* (London, John Wiley and Sons).

Sparkes, A.C. (1987) Strategic rhetoric: a constraint in changing the practice of teachers, *British Journal of Sociology of Education*, 8: 1, pp 37-54.

St.John-Brooks, C. (1983) 'English: a curriculum for personal development?', in: M. Hammersley and A. Hargreaves (Eds) *Curriculum Practice: Some Sociological Case Studies* (Lewes, Falmer Press).

Turner, G. (1983) 'The hidden curriculum of examinations', in: M. Hammersley and A. Hargreaves (Ed) *Curriculum Practice: Some Sociological Case Studies* (Lewes, Falmer Press).

Weston, P.B. (1979) *Negotiating the Curriculum: A Study in Secondary Schooling* (Windsor, NFER).

Printed in the United Kingdom for HMSO
Dd 300276 C10 4/95 3397 10170